FOR MYP

Community Project

Skills for Success

Laura England
Angela Stancar Johnson

FOR MYP
3 & 4

Community
Project

Skills for Success

Laura England
Angela Stancar Johnson

HODDER
EDUCATION
AN HACHETTE UK COMPANY

The Publishers would like to thank the following for permission to reproduce copyright material.

Photo credits

pp. viii–1, 8–9, 12–13, 31, 58, 71, 79, 97, 102–103, 107 © Jacob_09/Shutterstock; **p.60** *l* © Africa Studio/stock. adobe.com, *r* © Daisy Daisy/stock.adobe.com

Every effort has been made to trace all copyright holders, but if any have been inadvertently overlooked, the Publishers will be pleased to make the necessary arrangements at the first opportunity.

Acknowledgements

Laura – to her hardworking and remarkable colleagues at Good Shepherd Lutheran College.

Angela – to Adrian, Ella, Freya and Oskar.

The authors would like to acknowledge Good Shepherd Lutheran College and Southbank International School for some of the student resources used.

Bibliography

International Baccalaureate Organization, *IB Middle Years Programme Projects guide*, 2014, Geneva, Switzerland, International Baccalaureate Organization

International Baccalaureate Organization, *IB Middle Years Programme Further guidance for MYP projects*, 2016, Geneva, Switzerland, International Baccalaureate Organization

Brand, W. 2017, *Visual Thinking*, Amsterdam, Netherlands, BIS Publishers

Hoang, P and Taylor, C. 2017, *Extended essay for the IB Diploma*, London, UK, Hodder Education

Kleon, A. 2014, *Show Your Work*, New York, USA, Workman Publishing Company, Inc.

Ritchhart, R, Church, M and Morrison K. 2011, *Making Thinking Visible*, San Francisco, USA, Jossey-Bass

England, L. 2019, www.misslauraengland.blog/

Although every effort has been made to ensure that website addresses are correct at time of going to press, Hodder Education cannot be held responsible for the content of any website mentioned in this book.

Hachette UK's policy is to use papers that are natural, renewable and recyclable products and made from wood grown in well-managed forests and controlled sources. The logging and manufacturing processes are expected to conform to the environmental regulations of the country of origin.

Orders: please contact Hachette UK Distribution, Hely Hutchinson Centre, Milton Road, Didcot, Oxfordshire, OX11 7HH. Telephone: +44 (0)1235 827827. Email education@hachette.co.uk. Lines are open from 9 a.m. to 5 p.m., Monday to Saturday, with a 24-hour message answering service. You can also order through our website: www.hoddereducation.com

© Laura England and Angela Stancar Johnson 2019

First published in 2019 by
Hodder Education,
An Hachette UK Company
Carmelite House
50 Victoria Embankment
London EC4Y 0DZ

www.hoddereducation.com

Impression number 10 9 8 7 6 5 4 3

Year   2023 2022 2021

Cover photo © sdecoret - stock.adobe.com

Illustrations by Aptara Inc.

Typeset in India by Aptara Inc.

Printed in Spain

A catalogue record for this title is available from the British Library.

ISBN: 9781510463219

Contents

Introduction

How to use this book

Welcome to the community project for the IB MYP: Skills for Success.

This guide will help you prepare for your community project in an efficient and logical way.

Each chapter of the book looks at a different aspect of the project in detail, while practice exercises are also included to help you check your understanding, and put the guidance into practice.

To ensure *you* demonstrate *your* best work in the community project, this guide:

- includes an opening infographic in each chapter
- builds skills for success through a range of strategies and detailed expert advice, such as planning the best format for your presentation
- covers all the IB requirements with clear and concise explanations, such as the assessment criteria and rules on academic honesty
- demonstrates what is required to demonstrate your best work
- adds reference to the IB learner profile.

Key features of this guide include:

ATL skills

ATL skills covered are highlighted at the start of Chapters 2–10 and within each Activity. It is important to note that this is where you often have opportunities to demonstrate these skills, but they are not limited to these situations; any ATL skills can be demonstrated at any point.

LEARNER PROFILE ATTRIBUTES

Learner profile attributes are also highlighted at the start of Chapters 2–10.

EXPERT TIP

These tips appear throughout the book and provide guidance on steps you can take and key things you should consider in order to help you achieve your best.

ACTIVITY

Activities appear throughout the book, and provide you with the chance to put the skills and strategies into practice, to help you think about how to best approach your community project.

Supervisor check-in

Chapters 3–6 and 8 end with a checklist for your next supervisor meeting.

CHAPTER SUMMARY KEY POINTS

At the end of Chapters 1–8 and 10, key knowledge is distilled into a short checklist to help you review everything you have learned over the previous pages.

About the authors

Laura England is a Language & Literature and Design teacher at Good Shepherd Lutheran College in Darwin, Australia and is also a member of the Building Quality Curriculum reviewer team. Previously she was the MYP Coordinator and MYP Projects Coordinator for five years and during this time also served the Good Shepherd community of learners as Head of Design and Head of Language Acquisition. Prior to teaching Laura worked in advertising and co-owned and operated a photography business.

Angela Stancar Johnson is Head of English at Southbank International School in London, where she was previously the MYP Projects Coordinator. She has taught MYP Language & Literature, and DP English Literature and Language & Literature for the past nine years. Angela has in the past served as a moderator for the personal project and as an examiner for DP English and currently examines the MYP Interdisciplinary eAssessment. She also has experience in teaching high school journalism in the USA and has worked internationally in the scholastic publishing industry.

Laura and Angela co-authored *Personal Project for the IB MYP 4 & 5: Skills for Success* (Hodder Education, 2018).

Understanding the

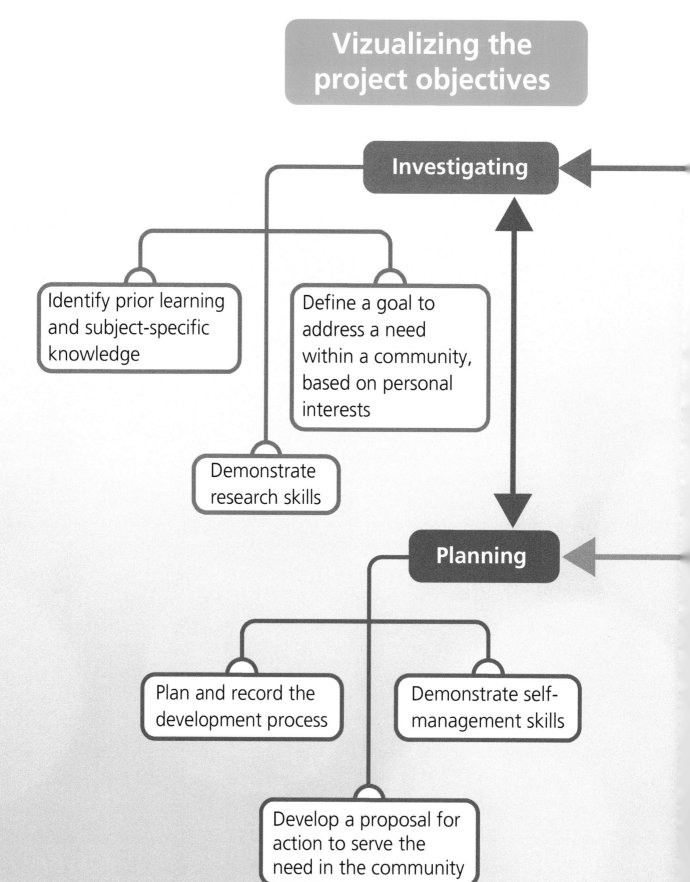

Investigating

Identify prior learning and subject-specific knowledge

Define a goal to address a need within a community, based on personal interests

Demonstrate research skills

Planning

Plan and record the development process

Demonstrate self-management skills

Develop a proposal for action to serve the need in the community

Community Project objectives

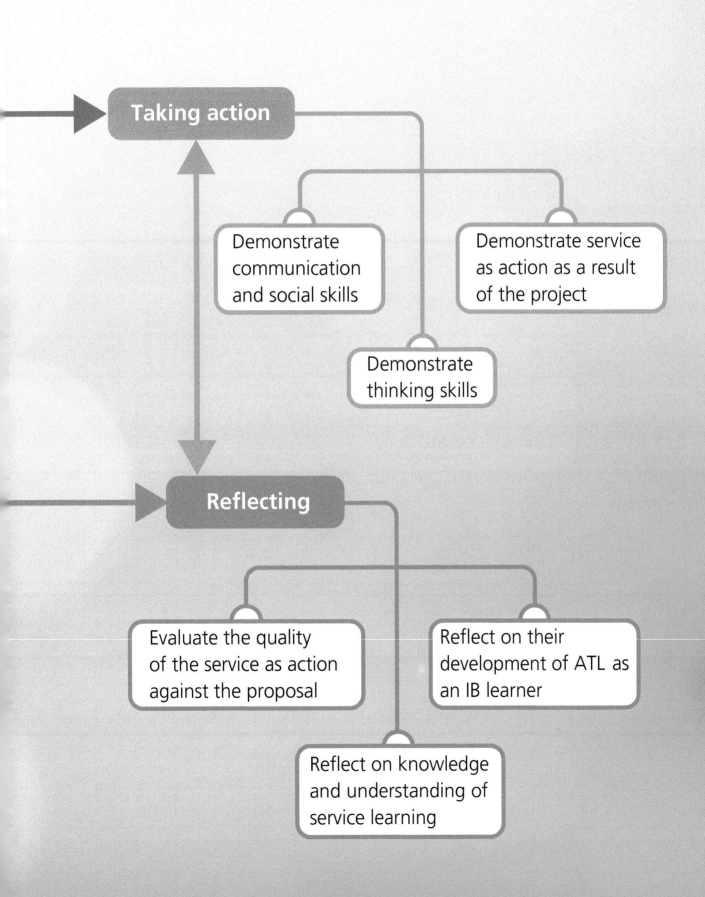

Understanding the Community Project objectives

What is the Community Project?

Welcome to the International Baccalaureate Middle Years Programme Community Project. The community project can form part of the core of your International Baccalaureate Middle Years Programme and can be a significant milestone in your journey as an IB learner.

The community project is a unique opportunity to use your strengths and skills to serve a community of your choosing. The community project is an exciting opportunity for you to develop awareness of needs in various communities and address those needs through service as action.

The community project allows you to apply your approaches to learning skills and apply how you learn best for the benefit of others. You will be given the opportunity to strengthen your approaches to learning skills, transfer prior learning and subject-specific knowledge into a new and perhaps unfamiliar situation, and implement service as action in a community of your choosing. If approached with the right mindset and a caring attitude, the community project can be a rewarding experience where you learn to exercise your privilege and responsibility to implement service as action in a community.

The community project consists of three parts:

- the process journal
- your participation in service as action
- the final presentation.

How to approach each of these parts will be covered in detail in the following chapters.

Community Project aims

Aims are general statements which relate to an overall goal or intended outcome. The community project aims state what you may expect to experience and learn through the process of service as action.

The aims of the MYP projects are to encourage and enable you to:

- participate in a sustained, self-directed inquiry within a global context
- generate creative new insights and develop deeper understandings through in-depth investigation
- demonstrate the skills, attitudes and knowledge required to complete a project over an extended period of time
- communicate effectively in a variety of situations
- demonstrate responsible action through, or as a result of, learning
- appreciate the process of learning and take pride in your accomplishments.

> **EXPERT TIP**
>
> It is important to note that the community project must not be linked to the curriculum or assessment of any of your subjects. However, the work you do in your subjects may support you in the development of your community project.

Community Project objectives

Objectives are specific steps along the journey towards the end goal. The community project objectives define what you will be able to accomplish as a result of your engagement. There are four main objectives, each of which align with the assessment criteria:

- Investigating
- Planning
- Taking action
- Reflecting.

Each objective is broken down further into three separate strands which relate to the overall objective.

Understanding the assessment criteria

The assessment criteria directly align with the community project objectives. Each criterion is worth a maximum of 8 levels. It is worth noting that a majority of the levels are awarded based on the process; only part of Criterion C directly assesses your participation in service as action. The tables below are taken from the community project assessment criteria.

The following information is taken directly from the IBO Projects guide. We recommend that as you read, replace the word 'student' with the personal pronouns of 'I' or 'we'. This will help you internalize and understand just what it is you can be aiming for in your community project.

Criterion A	
Investigating (8 levels)	
This is the starting point of your project. You start by investigating, but you may end up following the inquiry cycle (inquiry, action, reflection) more than once in order to strengthen, extend or refine your inquiry.	
Criterion A assesses your ability to:	
i define a goal to address a need within a community, based on personal interests	
ii identify prior learning and subject-specific knowledge relevant to the project	
iii demonstrate research skills.	
Achievement level	**Level descriptor**
0	Students **do not** achieve a standard described by any of the descriptors below.
1–2	Students: i **state** a goal to address a need within a community, based on personal interests, but this may be **limited** in depth or accessibility ii identify prior learning and subject-specific knowledge, but this may be **limited** in occurrence or relevance iii demonstrate **limited** research skills.

3–4	Students: i **outline** an **adequate** goal to address a need within a community, based on personal interests ii identify **basic** prior learning and subject-specific knowledge relevant to some areas of the project iii demonstrate **adequate** research skills.
5–6	Students: i **define a clear and challenging** goal to address a need within a community, based on personal interests ii identify prior learning and subject-specific knowledge **generally relevant** to the project iii demonstrate **substantial** research skills.
7–8	Students: i **define a clear and highly challenging** goal to address a need within a community, based on personal interests ii identify prior learning and subject-specific knowledge that is **consistently highly relevant** to the project iii demonstrate **excellent** research skills.

Criterion B
Planning (8 levels)
This includes all the work you will do to plan and organize your project towards participating in service as action. Criterion B assesses your ability to: i   develop a proposal for action to serve the need in the community ii   plan and record the development process of the project iii demonstrate self-management skills.

Achievement level	Level descriptor
0	Students **do not** achieve a standard described by any of the descriptors below.
1–2	Students: i develop a **limited** proposal for action to serve the need in the community ii present a **limited or partial** plan and record of the development process of the project iii demonstrate **limited** self-management skills.
3–4	Students: i develop an **adequate** proposal for action to serve the need in the community ii present an **adequate** plan and record of the development process of the project iii demonstrate **adequate** self-management skills.
5–6	Students: i develop a **suitable** proposal for action to serve the need in the community ii present a **substantial** plan and record of the development process of the project iii demonstrate **substantial** self-management skills.

7–8	Students:
	i develop a **detailed, appropriate and thoughtful** proposal for action to serve the need in the community
	ii present a **detailed and accurate** plan and record of the development process of the project
	iii demonstrate **excellent** self-management skills.

Criterion C
Taking action (8 levels)
This is the main 'doing' part of your project – the action part of the inquiry cycle – where you implement or participate in service as action.
Criterion C assesses your ability to:
i   demonstrate service as action as a result of the project
ii   demonstrate thinking skills
iii   demonstrate communication and social skills.

Achievement level	*Level descriptor*
0	Students **do not** achieve a standard described by any of the descriptors below.
1–2	Students:
	i demonstrate **limited** service as action as a result of the project
	ii demonstrate **limited** thinking skills
	iii demonstrate **limited** communication and social skills.
3–4	Students:
	i demonstrate **adequate** service as action as a result of the project
	ii demonstrate **adequate** thinking skills
	iii demonstrate **adequate** communication and social skills.
5–6	Students:
	i demonstrate **substantial** service as action as a result of the project
	ii demonstrate **substantial** thinking skills
	iii demonstrate **substantial** communication and social skills.
7–8	Students:
	i demonstrate **excellent** service as action as a result of the project
	ii demonstrate **excellent** thinking skills
	iii demonstrate **excellent** communication and social skills.

Criterion D
Reflecting (8 levels)
This is the point when you look back over the project and evaluate your development. You will have continuously reflected during the process of the community project and you can refer to this here too.
Criterion D assesses your ability to:
i   evaluate the quality of the service as action against the proposal
ii   reflect on how completing the project has extended your knowledge and understanding of service learning
iii   reflect on your development of ATL skills.

Achievement level	Level descriptor
0	Students **do not** achieve a standard described by any of the descriptors below.
1–2	Students: i present a **limited** evaluation of the quality of the service as action against the proposal ii present **limited** reflections on how completing the project has extended their knowledge and understanding of service learning iii present **limited** reflections on their development of ATL skills.
3–4	Students: i present an **adequate** evaluation of the quality of the service as action against the proposal ii present **adequate** reflections on how completing the project has extended their knowledge and understanding of service learning iii present **adequate** reflections on their development of ATL skills.
5–6	Students: i present a **substantial** evaluation of the quality of the service as action against the proposal ii present **substantial** reflections on how completing the project has extended their knowledge and understanding of service learning iii present **substantial** reflections on their development of ATL skills.
7–8	Students: i present an **excellent** evaluation of the quality of the service as action against the proposal ii present **excellent** reflections on how completing the project has extended their knowledge and understanding of service learning iii present **detailed and accurate** reflections on their development of ATL skills.

© International Baccalaureate Organization, *2014*

CHAPTER SUMMARY KEY POINTS

- The community project is an opportunity to use your strengths and approaches to learning skills to participate in service as action by meeting the needs of a community of your choice.

- The community project is a self-managed project that is not to be linked to any subject-specific curriculum or assessment.

- The community project consists of three parts:
  - the process journal
  - participation in service as action
  - the final presentation.

- You will be assessed on four criteria, each worth a maximum of 8 levels.

- The criteria you will be assessed on are:
  - Investigating
  - Planning
  - Taking action
  - Reflecting.

- Only Criterion C directly assesses your participation in service as action.

The community project can be completed independently, in pairs or in groups of three.

the Process Journal

The process journal can be presented in a variety of formats, either written, visual, audio – or a combination of all three.

Organization and the Process Journal

The community project is unique in that you may have a choice with regards to who you wish to work alongside as you engage in this service as action. The community project can be completed individually or collaboratively in groups of no more than three. Your school may set up the community project in a way that is most suitable for your context. There are two ways in which schools can set this up.

■ **School Process:** Your school may choose to ensure the community project is organized with partners and groups according to the organization of the MYP 3 or 4 cohort. This will be communicated to you via the allocated Projects Coordinator of your school for the community project.

■ **Self-Directed:** Your school may leave the choice of community project organization up to you. In this case, you may choose to complete the community project independently, with a partner or in a group of three.

Questions to consider when deciding how you wish to organize yourself before commencing the community project:

■ Is the service as action I wish to engage in better served by an individual, two people or a team of three?

■ Who else has the same commitment and enthusiasm to the community I wish to serve?

■ Who do I work well with?

■ Who has strengths that complement my own strengths?

■ Who has skills that I would like to acquire through learning from them?

■ Who can benefit from skills that I have in order for us to effectively serve others?

Remember, the community project is a sustained project that results in genuine and authentic service as action, so choose wisely who you will work with. Collaboration with the right team can benefit not only yourself as a learner, but also the community.

The Process Journal

The 'process journal' is a generic term used to refer to your self-maintained record of progress that you make throughout your community project journey. Before you begin your community project journey, you will need to organize a process journal.

EXPERT TIP

We often choose what is most familiar to us rather than taking risks to try new approaches. Use the community project as an opportunity to take a risk and work alongside classmates that you perhaps have not interacted much with so far. You may not only find new friends, but also discover a new set of skills and approaches to learning.

Documenting the process

The format of the process journal is completely up to you. Examples of what you may want to use are a notebook, online blog, iBook, Word document, OneNote book, visual art diary or a combination of formats – it is entirely up to you. Ensure that you backup your process journal continuously. The IBO has provided an outline of what the process journal is and is not.

The process journal is ...	The process journal is not ...
<ul><li>used throughout the project to document its development</li><li>an evolving record of intents, processes, accomplishments</li><li>a place to record initial thoughts and developments, brainstorming, possible lines of inquiry and further questions raised</li><li>a place for recording interactions with sources, for example, teachers, supervisors, external contributors</li><li>a place to record selected, annotated and/or edited research and to maintain a bibliography</li><li>a place for storing useful information, for example, quotations, pictures, ideas, photographs</li><li>a means of exploring ideas and solutions</li><li>a place for evaluation work completed</li><li>a place for reflecting on learning</li><li>devised by you, the student, in a format that suits your needs</li><li>a record of reflections and formative feedback received.</li></ul>	<ul><li>used on a daily basis (unless this is useful for your project)</li><li>written up after the process has been completed</li><li>additional work on top of the project; it is part of the project and supports the project</li><li>a diary with detailed writing about what was done</li><li>a static document with only one format.</li></ul>

© International Baccalaureate Organization, *2014*

The community project is a creative and compassionate endeavour. You are participating in something truly unique and important. Throughout this book, consistent reference is made to your process journal. Make sure your process journal clearly communicates the particular objectives you are addressing, or the ATL skill you are using or reflecting on. You will see examples of most of the community project objectives in the following chapters – these are examples of what can be evident in your own process journal. For example, in your process journal, you may reflect on a point of conflict resolution that you engaged in. Using a comment or a highlighter, it is a good idea to simply identify what objective you are addressing and what ATL skill you have employed. In this example, you can identify this as a social-collaboration skill that is part of Criterion C: Taking action. This approach can support your supervisor by identifying how you are developing your ATL skills and also ensures that you address each of the community project objectives.

CHAPTER SUMMARY KEY POINTS

- The community project can be completed alone, with a partner or in a group of three. Choose wisely how to organize yourself for the community project.

- Before you start your community project, organize your process journal format(s).

- Make sure you use your process journal to make your community project journey visible and understand your process of participating in service as action.

Identities and relationships

Fairness and development

Orientation in space and time

The global context is the lens through which you view, or approach, your project

Globalization and sustainability

Personal and cultural expression

Scientific and technical innovation

Investigating

> ## ■ ATL skills
>
> - ■ Communication skills
> - ■ Critical-thinking skills
> - ■ Organization skills
> - ■ Creative-thinking skills
> - ■ Information literacy skills
> - ■ Transfer skills
> - ■ Media literacy skills
> - ■ Affective skills
> - ■ Collaboration skills

LEARNER PROFILE ATTRIBUTES		
Inquirers	Caring	Thinkers
Communicators	Knowledgeable	Principled

The community

In order to effectively implement or participate in service as action, you must learn about the community you are serving. This is called service learning, or service as action. Essentially, it means learning about a community in order to serve them to the best of your ability.

Although the community project is organized through using your approaches to learning skills, strengths and interests to engage in service as action, the community project is ultimately about others. It requires you to care about a community and develop empathy skills in order to meet the needs of others. Within this chapter, you will be equipped with the skills to effectively learn about the community you have chosen and how you can best engage with this community in order to serve them in a meaningful and empowering manner.

■ Focus on something that interests you

We always learn and serve best when what we are engaging in is important to us. The community project gives you an opportunity to explore and serve others within an area that is of interest to you. It might be helpful to read the questions below and reflect on your skills and interests. If you are working in a pair or a group of three, simply consider the question as a group question to respond to. These are questions that you can discuss and, through collaboration, respond accordingly.

> ### ACTIVITY: WHAT INTERESTS ME?
>
> In your process journal, begin to brainstorm the following questions:
> - ■ What interests me?
> - ■ What am I passionate about?
> - ■ What communities am I interested in learning about?
> - ■ What communities am I interested in serving?
> - ■ What could I commit to over a long time period that will keep me engaged and interested?

Defining a need within a community

Before you launch into developing a goal to address a need within a community, let's establish a clear understanding of the terminology we will be using in order to develop this goal.

▨ What is a need?

A need can be defined as:

▨ a condition or situation in which something is required or wanted for a community to flourish

▨ a duty or obligation

▨ something that is desirable or useful.

▨ What is a community?

The community may be local, national, virtual or global. There is a wide range of definitions of community. The MYP key concept of community is defined as follows:

> Communities are groups that exist in proximity defined by space, time or relationship. Communities include, for example, groups of people sharing particular characteristics, beliefs or values as well as groups of interdependent organisms living together in a specific habitat.

MYP: From principles into practice (May 2014)

Here are some examples of the various types of communities from the IBO Projects guide:

Community	Examples		
A group of people living in the same place	Singapore's Indian neighbourhood	Belgian citizens	Korowai people of Papua
A group of people sharing particular characteristics, beliefs and/or values	An online forum for people with Down's syndrome	Vegetarians	History club Year 3 students
A body of nations or states unified by common interests	European Union	United States of America	United Nations Human Rights Council
A group of interdependent plants or animals growing or living together in a specified habitat	Madagascar's indigenous bird population	Flora of the Middle East in Western Asia	South Korea's Ecorium project (wetland reserve)

When considering a community to serve, think very carefully about how you might specifically address needs in this community. Consider the following questions:

▨ Do I have access to the resources I would need to serve the community effectively?

▨ Is there a sufficient amount of information available regarding this community so I can truly learn about them?

▨ Can I acquire enough knowledge to serve the community within the time frame allotted and to the best of my ability?

Your turn:

With this foundational terminology established, and your brainstorm about your interests and passions completed, it is your turn to choose the community that you wish to serve through the community project.

Thinking about your community

ACTIVITY: SWOT CHART

■ ATL skills

- Information literacy skills
  - Collect and analyse data to identify solutions and make informed decisions
- Critical-thinking skills
  - Practise observing carefully in order to recognize problems
  - Draw reasonable conclusions and generalizations

A good place to start when considering the needs of the community that you have chosen is through the use of a SWOT chart that focuses on the community overall.

In your process journal, create a SWOT chart template, like the one below, and use the following guiding questions to think deeply about this community.

Consider the following question prompts:
- Strengths – what are the strengths of this community?
- Weaknesses – what are the weaknesses in this community?
- Opportunities – what opportunities are available for you to serve this community?
- Threats – what external or internal obstacles will you face in serving this community?

Strengths	Weaknesses
Opportunities	Threats

■ Addressing a need

Now that you have started to think about the community, let's narrow our thinking of this community into deciding on one need to address within this community.

To help you think deeply about the chosen need within this community, a good place to start is using a SOAR chart.

A SOAR chart is similar to the SWOT chart; however, it becomes much more focused on setting a clear goal.

SWOT: Evaluating the community

SOAR: Need within the community

ACTIVITY: SOAR CHART

■ ATL skills

- Creative-thinking skills
  - Use brainstorming and visual diagrams to generate new ideas and inquiries
- Critical-thinking skills
  - Draw reasonable conclusions and generalizations
- Affective skills
  - Practise positive thinking

In your process journal, create a SOAR chart template and use the prompting questions opposite to consider the specific needs of this community.

Consider the following question prompts:
- Strengths – what is already underway to meet the need you have chosen? What is already working well to meet the need within this community?
- Opportunities – what opportunities are there for you to meet this need? Is anything not working well to meet the need within this community?
- Aspirations – what would you like to achieve through meeting this need?
- Results – what results will you look for to know your service has been successful?

Strengths	Weaknesses
Aspirations	Results

With this developing understanding of the community and the need you have chosen to address, you should consider the type of service that you will engage in throughout the community project.

Types of service

Service is expressed in multiple ways and the purpose is always to meet the needs of others. Now that you have chosen a community to serve and have identified a need within this community, consider the approach in which you will serve. The approach you choose for your community project is the type of service that will provide you with the best possible opportunity to meet the need in the community.

Read through the types of service below and, in your process journal, identify the type of service you plan to engage in and explain why this type of service is essential to you meeting the need within the community you have chosen.

This is an interaction that involves people, the environment or animals.

You do not see the community you are serving during indirect service; however, you can verify that your actions will benefit the community and the environment.

Through advocacy, you speak on behalf of a cause or concern to promote action on an issue of public interest.

You collect information through varied sources, analyse data and report on a topic of importance to influence policy or practice.

Remember to consider your personal strengths and interests when deciding on the type of service you wish to engage in.

Establish the goal

In order for the community's aspirations to be met and the results of your service as action to be evident, consider how you might place this into an achievable, rewarding and highly challenging goal. The community project is an important project that requires lots of deep thinking, collaboration and self-motivation. You need to make sure that your goal is highly challenging and that it will extend you and help you grow as a caring and self-managed learner.

> **EXPERT TIP**
>
> When choosing a type of service for your community project, it is a good idea to consider your resources. Make sure you have the resources to meet the identified need in this community to the best of your ability.

Here are some examples of goals that have been further developed to grow from a challenging goal to a highly challenging goal.

Challenging goal	Highly challenging goal
You may recognize an issue of cyber-bullying among your school community and raise awareness through an information campaign.	You may instigate a change in the disciplinary procedures taken against cyber-bullying among school peers, through negotiations with various school stakeholders such as teachers, student leadership council, heads of school, etc.
You may hear that the local children's hospital is understaffed and volunteer your services for a set period of time.	You create a puppet show to entertain children and to tour several schools and hospitals.
You may think your school needs to support a local autism society next door to the campus, so you design and create a children's story to educate your peers on what autism is.	You may work with the autism society members to write and publish a children's story together, which is then showcased at the school's open day, hosted by students and society members.
You may raise awareness of the need for blood donation at a local hospital or clinic.	You may organize a blood drive to be held at your school during student-led conferences.

ACTIVITY: EXTENSION SCAFFOLD

ATL skills

- Organization skills
  - Set goals that are challenging and realistic
- Critical-thinking skills
  - Practise observing carefully in order to recognize opportunities

In your process journal, create an Extension Scaffold that can help you extend the features of a challenging goal into a highly challenging goal.

Place in the first column an ATL skill that is required for a challenging goal, extend this by including a complementary and more advanced skill to the centre column. Once you have combined these two together, consider just how these two working together will create an opportunity for a highly challenging goal.

Consider the following question prompts:

- What ATL skills are required in a challenging goal, and what ATL skills are required in a highly challenging goal?
- How many members of a community are impacted in a challenging goal and how many members of a community are impacted in a highly challenging goal?
- If possible, how is the community invited to participate in the challenging goal, and how is the community invited to participate in the highly challenging goal?

Challenging goal	Highly challenging goal	Combined and transferred
Skill required for a challenging goal +	Add to this skill by thinking of how = it may be extended through extending the required skill	Draw the skills together and consider how they can be transferred to a highly challenging goal
Example		
Practising positive thinking	Practising resilience + positive thinking	The goal will require more than a one-off attempt; it will require a process and persistence that will need resilience through maintaining positive thinking.

Now that you have chosen the community you will serve, the need within this community that you will endeavour to meet, and you have the knowledge of what makes a highly challenging goal, take a risk and create your own highly challenging goal.

Reflect on what you discovered were the features of a highly challenging goal in comparison to a challenging goal and make sure your goal has those same features of multiple ATL skills, impact on members of the community, and community participation.

Defining a context

A global context provides a framework for your community project and connects your goal to a specific area of need that is relevant to all global citizens. A global context also provides different perspectives on your community project. Have a look at the list of global contexts below and using the global context perspectives lens consider how your community project goal can be connected to one of these contexts.

Questions to consider as you read through the global contexts:

- How can this global context help others understand just how important it is to address this need within the community?
- How can this global context cause others to care about this community?
- How can this global context connect others to this community project?

Global context	Examples of community projects
Identities and relationships You will explore identity; beliefs and values; personal, physical, mental, social and spiritual health; human relationships including families, friends, communities and cultures; what it means to be human.	• Laughter therapy campaign in children's hospital or care home for the elderly • Tutoring classes providing additional or special instruction to primary school students • Researching the effects of cola drinks on digestion and developing a campaign to promote healthy choices available from school vending machines
Orientation in space and time You will explore personal histories; homes and journeys; turning points in humankind; discoveries; explorations and migrations of humankind; the relationships between and the interconnectedness of individuals and civilizations from personal, local and global perspectives.	• Joining a museum or historical society in the community to contribute to maintaining, restoring and recording the local history • Making a plan for wheelchair accessibility • Inspired by the lack of facilities in the local community, seeking to improve the facilities for young people by producing an article for the school magazine summarizing the problem and possible solutions
Personal and cultural expression You will explore the ways in which we discover and express ideas, feelings, nature, culture, beliefs and values; the ways in which we reflect on, extend and enjoy our creativity; our appreciation of the aesthetic.	• Improving the environment in the local hospital by designing and creating a series of pictures to hang in the corridors • Performing a theatre play to raise awareness of bullying • Promoting intercultural understanding through a graffiti contest

Global context	Examples of community projects
Scientific and technical innovation You will explore the natural world and its laws; the interaction between people and the natural world; how humans use their understanding of scientific principles; the impact of scientific and technological advances on communities and environments; the impact of environments on human activity; how humans adapt environments to their needs.	● Helping a local community make an efficient, low-cost use of energy-powered devices ● Developing a programme to promote the use of wind energy for domestic devices ● Campaigning to reduce paper use and to promote recycling ● Campaigning to reduce water, electricity or fuel waste
Globalization and sustainability You will explore the interconnectedness of human-made systems and communities; the relationship between local and global processes; how local experiences mediate the global; the opportunities and tensions provided by world-interconnectedness; the impact of decision-making on humankind and the environment.	● Campaigning to raise awareness and reduce plastic straw use ● Passing a plan to local authorities for tree planting in an area in need of re-greening ● Creating a school or community garden
Fairness and development You will explore rights and responsibilities; the relationship between communities; sharing finite resources with other people and with other living things; access to equal opportunities; peace and conflict resolution.	● Campaigning for fair-trade awareness ● Contributing to educational opportunities, for example, supporting a local non-governmental organization that works on literacy ● Addressing the concerns of immigrants and migrant populations

ACTIVITY: GLOBAL CONTEXT PERSPECTIVES LENS

■ ATL skills

■ Transfer skills
  • Change the context of an inquiry to gain different perspectives

In your process journal, create the global context perspectives lens scaffold in order to structure your thinking about the various perspectives each of the global contexts provide your community project goal.

Thinking deeply through the lens of each of the six global contexts, explore how your community project goal can be extended by each of these global contexts.

Consider the following question prompts:
■ How might this global context give my community project a wider sphere of influence?
■ How might this global context help others understand just how important it is to meet the need in this community?
■ How might this global context cause others to care about the need in this community?

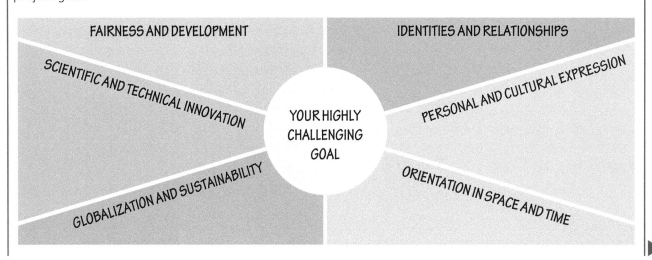

Here is an example of a student's global perspectives lens on their goal.

FAIRNESS AND DEVELOPMENT

As my peers feel that this unexpected loss is unfair and they are struggling to understand why this has happened, I could focus the *Book of Smiles* to explore healthy ways to navigate this feeling of deep injustice.

IDENTITIES AND RELATIONSHIPS

The *Book of Smiles* can explore how supportive relationships can help the process of grief and loss in a humorous way so the *Book of Smiles* brings both instructional information and also brings a smile to the face of my peers.

SCIENTIFIC AND TECHNICAL INNOVATION

I could focus on the scientific principles of processing grief and loss. I can then choose the most relevant of these principles for my classmates and create a humorous narrative that provides my peers with scientific facts as well as a quirky story to help them in this process of grief and loss.

YOUR HIGHLY CHALLENGING GOAL

Last year my peers and I experienced deep grief and loss with the passing of a good friend. My community project goal is to engage in research of what creates positive emotions that I can creatively transfer into a *Book of Smiles*. The artwork in the *Book of Smiles* will be created by myself, and is to be professionally printed and given to each of the classes in my cohort to help my peers cope with grief and loss through experiencing positive emotions.

PERSONAL AND CULTURAL EXPRESSION

The focus of the *Book of Smiles* can be on how the psychology of working through grief can be connected to specific aesthetics and this expression of psychology through aesthetics can support my peers in this process of grief and loss.

GLOBALIZATION AND SUSTAINABILITY

The *Book of Smiles* can specifically focus on the role of nature in helping people process grief and loss. I can create characters that humorously show the journey of processing grief and loss and how nature supports this process. This can include a powerful message of the need to work collectively to ensure a sustainable future for our world.

ORIENTATION IN SPACE AND TIME

I can create the main message in the *Book of Smiles* to not only help my peers smile in times of grief and loss but to also be encouraged that over time this deep sadness won't feel as painful as it does now.

Once you have selected one global context that you believe best suits your community project goal and allows others to understand just how important your service is, consider how you may need to adjust your goal. Do you need to include a different perspective provided by the chosen global context?

To be really sure that your community project goal is not only highly challenging but also well considered, appropriate and thoughtful, at this point it is a good idea to conduct a Circle of Viewpoints. The Circle of Viewpoints visible thinking routine provides a scaffold in which you can ensure that the way in which you intend to meet the need in the chosen community considers multiple perspectives.

ACTIVITY: CIRCLE OF VIEWPOINTS

■ ATL skills

- ■ Critical-thinking skills
  - • Consider ideas from multiple perspectives
  - • Use models to explore complex systems and issues
- ■ Collaboration skills
  - • Practise empathy

- ■ I am thinking of … *[impact of the community project goal]* from the point of view of …
- ■ I think … *[describe the impact from your chosen viewpoint. Be an actor – take on the character of your viewpoint]*. Because … *[explain your reasoning]*
- ■ A question/concern I have from this viewpoint is …

Draw up the following scaffold in your process journal and consider your community project goal from the perspective of a person or group of people impacted by your service.

You may find that you need to conduct more than one Circle of Viewpoint in order to gather a more thorough picture of the possible points of view on your community project goal. **You may find that you need to adjust your community project goal as a result of this activity. This is absolutely okay as the community project cycle is interactive and each part impacts the other and requires reflection and adjustment. Just like a community.**

I am thinking of …
from the point of
view of …

Community
project goal:

Questions/
concerns I have
from this
viewpoint are …

I think …
Because …

■ Highly challenging goal reflection – skills

In order to ensure that your community project goal is indeed a highly challenging goal, consider the questions opposite. The questions guide your thinking to consider how your community project goal will provide you with an opportunity to demonstrate each of the approaches to learning skills.

How does your community project goal provide you with an opportunity to …

… exchange thoughts, messages and information effectively through interacting with others?

… read, write and use your language skills to gather information and communicate information?

… work effectively with others?

… manage your time and project effectively?

… manage your state of mind and wellbeing?

… reflect on the process of meeting the need in the community you have chosen?

… find, interpret, judge and create information?

… interact with different media to use and create ideas and information?

… analyse and evaluate issues and ideas?

… generate novel ideas and consider new perspectives?

… use skills and knowledge in multiple situations?

■ Highly challenging goal reflection – IB learner

In order to ensure that your community project goal is indeed a highly challenging goal, consider the questions below. The questions guide your thinking to consider how your community project goal will provide you with an opportunity to continue to strive to embody the characteristics of the IB learner profile attributes.

How does your community project goal provide you with an opportunity to …

… continue to strive to be an inquirer?

… continue to strive to be a knowledgeable learner?

… continue to strive to be a thinker?

… continue to strive to be a communicator?

... continue to strive to be a principled learner?

... continue to strive to be an open-minded learner?

... continue to strive to be a caring learner?

... continue to strive to be a risk-taker?

... continue to strive to be balanced?

... continue to strive to be reflective?

Identify prior learning and subject-specific knowledge

▣ Identify prior learning

Now that you have developed a highly challenging goal based on personal interest and have connected this goal to an MYP global context, you now need to identify prior learning that will help you achieve your goal.

ACTIVITY: PRIOR LEARNING REFLECTION

▣ ATL skills

- Transfer skills
  - Apply skills and knowledge in unfamiliar situations

Think about the skills and knowledge that you already have from clubs, training, independent learning, family hobbies, skills you have learned outside of school and all other forms of learning that you have engaged in that will help you achieve your community project goal. If you are working with a partner or in a group this means that you will have multiple elements of prior learning that will help you achieve your goal.

In your community project process journal, you can create the following table, or you can simply jot down ideas in an approach of your choice.

Prior learning *(For example, clubs, training, online courses, programmes, etc.)*	Explain how this prior learning will help you achieve your community project goal. *(Explain in detail the specific prior learning that you can transfer to achieving your community project goal.)*	What additional learning do you need to acquire in order to achieve your community project goal? *(Explain what additional learning you need to acquire in order to achieve your community project goal.)*

▣ Identify subject-specific knowledge

Building on from prior learning, you now need to think about what you have learned through inquiry-based learning experiences in all your subjects and how that can help you achieve your community project goal.

ACTIVITY: SUBJECT-SPECIFIC KNOWLEDGE REFLECTION

■ ATL skills

- Transfer skills
  - Apply skills and knowledge in unfamiliar situations

Think deeply about the skills you are acquiring or have mastered from your learning, the subject-specific knowledge that you have gathered and the attitudes towards learning that you have developed in your classes.

In your community project process journal, you can create the following table, or you can simply jot down ideas in an approach of your choice.

MYP subject-specific skills and knowledge *(For example, Language and Literature: Features of a visual text for a film creation; Design – Engineering and Robotics: Programming for game creation, etc.)*	How will these skills and knowledge help you achieve your community project goal? *(Explain in detail how you can transfer these skills and knowledge to achieving your community project goal. For example, if you are making a short movie about helping refugees settle into a new city, the film-making skills and film analysis skills you have acquired in Language and Literature can be transferred to helping you achieve your community project goal.)*

Demonstrate research skills

Building on from your reflection and explanation of your prior learning and subject-specific knowledge, begin to think about just what further knowledge and skills you need in order to achieve your community project goal.

Research skills essential for community project success include:

■ Media literacy

■ Information literacy.

Media literacy skills involve interacting with media to use and create ideas and information. As you engage in the Investigating process you will find, organize, analyse, evaluate, synthesize and ethically use information from a variety of sources and media. This includes digital social media and online networks.

A significant part of the media literacy skills required for the community project is to seek a range of perspectives from multiple and varied sources. It is important to analyze the accuracy of the sources you are using by seeking varied perspectives from other sources. This will enable you to make informed decisions regarding the accuracy of the source through making connections between the information presented in varied sources.

Information literacy skills involve finding, interpreting, judging and creating information. As you engage in the Investigating process you will access information to be informed about how to best serve the need in the community you have chosen. You will also collect information, compare the information you have collected and through this comparison determine the best solution for addressing the identified need in the community. Being a principled learner and creating a bibliography of all the sources you have employed to place your community project goal into action is another way in which you will develop and strengthen you information literacy skills.

ACTIVITY: KNOWLEDGE AND SKILLS RESEARCH QUESTIONS

ATL skills

- Organization skills
  - Set goals that are challenging and realistic
- Transfer skills
  - Apply skills and knowledge in unfamiliar situations

In your process journal, you can draw the following table that provides a scaffold for how you can outline just what you know and what you need to know in order to achieve your goal.

Knowledge:

What knowledge do I already have of how to achieve my community project goal?	What knowledge do I need to gain in order to achieve my community project goal?	How can I find this information? Where can I find this information? Who can support me in the search for new knowledge?

Skills:

What skills do I already have to achieve my community project goal?	What skills do I need to gain in order to achieve my community project goal?	How can I find information on how to develop these skills? Where can I find support and coaching? Who is an expert who can teach me the skills I need to acquire?

Convert the knowledge and skills that you need to acquire (middle column) in order to successfully achieve your community project goal into inquiry questions that can guide your research.

Document your inquiry questions in your process journal and ensure that they have direct relevance to achieving your community project goal and effectively serving the community you have chosen. As you progress throughout the community project inquiry cycle, you will find that many other inquiry questions arise – continue to add these questions as you progress.

EXPERT TIP

Quality inquiry questions are essential for quality research. Make sure your inquiry questions are focused and allow you to gather information that you can transfer directly to putting your community project goal into action.

Primary and secondary sources

Research is about connecting with sources in order to gather specific information. Make sure you gather information from both primary and secondary sources. Primary sources might include, but are not limited to, images, interviews, survey data, results of experiments or fieldwork. Secondary sources might include books, websites, journal articles or other published media. Depending on the type of project you undertake, you will likely use a combination of primary and secondary sources. There is no set number of sources which you must use as this will depend on the nature of the project itself.

Employing your communication and social skills, take risks and connect with primary sources in the community – there is a wealth of knowledge and skills to be gained beyond your classroom walls.

Book a time to meet with the Library team so they can support you in your research of secondary sources – the Teacher Librarian is the school research guru! Their help can be superb. To support you as you engage in the research process it is a good idea to check out Chapter 8: Academic honesty (see page 98). Here we have outlined approaches to practising academic honesty and discuss the requirements of your bibliography.

EXPERT TIP

It is a really good idea to create your bibliography continuously as you progress through your community project so you can accurately acknowledge sources you have used. There are multiple online sources that provide you with the tools to generate a bibliography. Liaise with your school's Teacher Librarian for the best possible online source to support you in developing a comprehensive bibliography.

Remember to be principled and in all your interactions be respectful. Ensure that all who you interact with are treated with dignity.

Research is a continual process throughout the community project. You will find as you work towards achieving your community project goal that research is an essential element of each section of the community project inquiry cycle.

When engaging in research for the community project you need to focus on the following skills:

- Summarizing information
- Analysing information
- Transferring information
- Practising academic honesty.

To help you with this process, you can create the following scaffolds in your process journal or you can choose a different approach – it is up to you.

Currency

When was the information published or posted?

Has the information been changed or updated?

Does your community project goal require current information, or will older sources work just as well?

Transfer

How will you use and transfer this information in order to achieve your community project goal?

Relevancy

Does the information in this source relate directly to your community project goal and sufficiently answer this inquiry question?

Who is the intended audience?

Accuracy

Is the information in this source supported by evidence?

Has the author provided references?

Is the information unbiased and free of emotion?

Can you easily identify spelling and punctuation errors?

Authority

Who is the author/publisher of this source?

Is the author/publisher qualified to share information on this topic?

If this is a website, does the url reveal anything about the author or source? For example, .gov, .org.

Purpose

What is the author/publisher's purpose for sharing this information? Is it to sell, teach, inform, entertain or persuade?

Is the information factual, opinion or propaganda?

Are there cultural, political, religious or personal biases?

Inquiry question:				
Name of source:				
Location /url:			Date accessed:	
Summary notes:				
-				
-				
-				
-				
-				
Currency:	Relevancy:	Accuracy:	Authority:	Purpose:
Transfer:				

Enjoy the process of research! Make sure your research and analysis is clearly visible in your process journal throughout the project and enjoy making new discoveries and mastering new skills.

■ Surveys

Another way for you to demonstrate excellent research skills is through surveys. You may find that in order to gather as much data and information as possible on just how to effectively meet the need in the community you have chosen, your community project may benefit from conducting a survey.

There are several steps to take in developing an effective survey:

Step 1: Choose your target audience wisely

Consider the following questions:

- Who can give me the most accurate information?
- Who is impacted by the need in the community I have chosen?
- Who will give me honest information?

Step 2: Develop your survey questions

Here are some tips for developing quality survey questions:

- Write questions that are simple and direct.
- Use simple words for clear communication.
- Limit the number of ranking options. For example, it is often challenging to respond to a 10-point survey ranking, when the answer could easily be provided using a Strongly Agree – Agree – Disagree – Strongly Disagree scale.
- If you are using a multiple-choice question format, address all the options without any doubling up.
- To gather a wide range of feedback, it is a good idea to use different types of questions. For example, multiple-choice, true or false, agree or disagree, short answer and long answer types of questions.

Step 3: Choose survey software

There are multiple online programs and apps that provide you with quality tools for surveys. You may find that a survey conducted face-to-face using a paper copy of the survey attached to a clipboard suits you best. Choose the approach that best suits your learning style and your community project goal.

Step 4: Double-check, edit, fix

Make sure your survey does not have errors. Double-check and amend any errors.

Step 5: Engage your target audience

Send or deliver your survey. Make sure you place a closing date and time for your survey so you can collect the data in a time-efficient and organized manner.

Step 6: Analyse the data

When the data from your survey is in and you have an overall visualization of the data and information collected, consider just what to do with this data and information. The following questions can be considered when thinking about just how you can apply this information to your community project:

■ What does this information show me about my community project goal?

■ What does this information tell me about the way in which I am planning to address the need in the community I have chosen?

■ How can I transfer this first-hand information from the target audience I have identified to my community project goal?

Supervisor Check-in

■ Share your initial ideas with your supervisor. Your supervisor may be able to help you narrow your ideas down to a focused, specific goal.
■ Discuss with your supervisor how you might focus your community project through the different global context lenses. Which one seems most appropriate for your goal?
■ Discuss the prior learning and subject-specific knowledge you have identified and gather feedback on how this can be transferred to your community project goal.
■ Share your process journal with your supervisor.
■ Share your research with your supervisor and gather feedback on your approach to demonstrating academic honesty.

A great tool to use when considering how you can communicate your community project goal is through a Compass Points visible thinking routine. You could have this prepared and ready for your meeting with your supervisor and use this as a flow for how you will discuss your project thus far.

ACTIVITY: KNOWLEDGE AND SKILLS RESEARCH QUESTIONS

ATL skills

■ Organization skills
  • Set goals that are challenging and realistic
  • Plan strategies and take action to achieve personal and academic goals
■ Transfer skills
  • Inquire in different contexts to gain a different perspective
■ Communication skills
  • Negotiate ideas and knowledge with peers and teachers

In your process journal, draw a compass and consider the following questions:

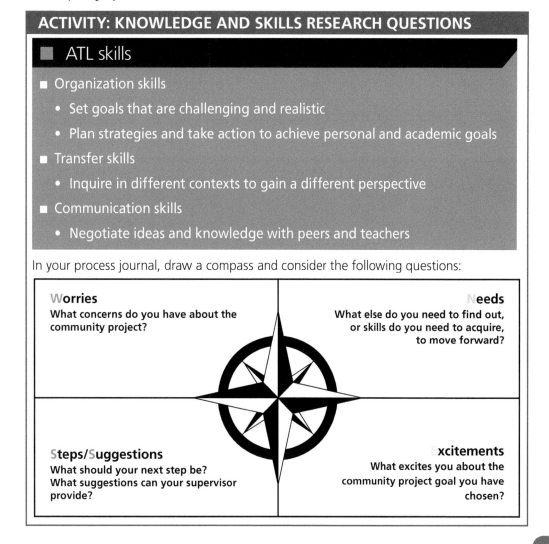

Worries
What concerns do you have about the community project?

Needs
What else do you need to find out, or skills do you need to acquire, to move forward?

Steps/**S**uggestions
What should your next step be? What suggestions can your supervisor provide?

Excitements
What excites you about the community project goal you have chosen?

CHAPTER SUMMARY KEY POINTS

- The first objective of the community project is investigating.

- The first step in investigating is to define a need within a community and define a clear and highly challenging goal to meet the need of this community through service.

- To frame this goal, you need to select one global context in which to focus your community project. You can choose from:
  - Identities and relationships
  - Orientation in space and time
  - Personal and cultural expression
  - Scientific and technical innovation
  - Globalization and sustainability
  - Fairness and development.

- You should identify prior learning and subject-specific knowledge that you have gained within the MYP classroom and outside of the classroom that you can bring with you to the community project to help you place your goal into action.

- The community project provides you with an opportunity to demonstrate research skills and through the information you discover, develop your approaches to learning skill of transfer by transferring this information to your community project.

Planning

It is important to carefully plan each stage of your community project. You will need to use **affective**, **cognitive** and **metacognitive** skills to do this.

AFFECTIVE SKILLS

Affective skills include your ability to manage your own time and be self-motivated, as well as being focused, resilient and persevering.

COGNITIVE SKILLS

Cognitive skills include your memory, problem-solving and attention skills.

METACOGNITIVE SKILLS

Metacognitive skills are essential for planning, as they include thinking about how to approach a task, strategies for problem-solving and self-assessment.

Planning

At this stage in the community project process you have:

- ■ defined a goal to address a need within a community based on personal interest
- ■ identified prior learning and subject-specific knowledge relevant to the project, and you have explained how this can be transferred to your project and serve as a foundation for research and transfer
- ■ started to engage in both primary and secondary research and have demonstrated how you are a principled learner by practising academic honesty.

The next step is to develop a detailed, appropriate and thoughtful proposal for action that will further outline how you will achieve your goal and effectively meet the need of the community you have identified.

Before we move into how to develop a proposal for action, let's elaborate on the language of the criteria.

- ■ **Detailed:** Detailed means you demonstrate an attention to detail. You think deeply about the action you wish to take to serve the need in the community. You think from multiple perspectives and take your time to thoroughly understand the need and consider the most respectful and principled approach to service.
- ■ **Appropriate:** Appropriate means suitable for the circumstances. Your proposal for action shows that you have carefully considered how your service is suitable for the circumstances of the community. You show you have carefully thought about the impact of your service.
- ■ **Thoughtful:** Thoughtful means you have thought very carefully about the needs of others. Your proposal for action demonstrates an understanding of the needs of the community and also demonstrates the kind of thinking that looks beyond the surface to the reasons. When you are demonstrating thoughtful considerations, you may find yourself asking questions that begin with 'why' and 'what if ...'

Develop a proposal for action to serve the need in the community

In order to create your proposal for action, you need to take the time to be thoughtful and consider how you can create a detailed and appropriate proposal. To support you in your thinking, you can think deeply about the following community-specific factors. Remember, you may have other community-specific factors beyond these, so add these and think just as deeply about them.

Community-specific factors	Guiding questions
Cultural understanding	Do you need to consider differences in culture and how these can be respected and celebrated in your community project?
Environmental considerations	Do you need to consider the impact your community project will have on the natural environment?
Human rights and dignity	How will you ensure that human rights and dignity are respected as you engage in meeting the need in this community? Are you able to promote equality through your community project?
Animal welfare	Do you need to consider animal welfare?
Community factors	What unique factors of the community do you need to consider?
Sensitivity and empathy	How will you remain sensitive to the needs of those impacted by the need in the community you are serving? How can you develop and demonstrate empathy?
Language needs	Do you need to consider language needs and language barriers? How will you make sure language needs are met?

In your process journal, document how you think deeply about the community-specific factors that are essential for you to create a detailed, appropriate and thoughtful proposal for action.

ACTIVITY: LOTUS DIAGRAM

■ ATL skills

- ■ Collaboration skills
  - Practise empathy
- ■ Critical-thinking skills
  - Draw reasonable conclusions and generalizations

A great tool to use to visualize your thinking is a Lotus Diagram. In the centre of the Lotus Diagram scaffold, place your community project goal. Around the outside in the boxes connected to the goal, jot down the community-specific factors that you need to make in order to create your detailed, appropriate and thoughtful proposal for action.

In the corresponding boxes connected to the community-specific factor, you can jot down questions that can guide your deep thinking or responses to how you will address this factor in your community project.

			Community Project Goal					

Here is an example of a student's Lotus Diagram, using the highly challenging community project goal of:
My community project goal is to create a Public Service Announcement (PSA) that advocates for the reversal of the local fracking policy, through education of the realities of fracking and providing the audience with options for how they can take action and join the anti-fracking advocacy movement.

				The spiritual connection to the land	Historical connection to the land			
				Cultural Understanding	Way of life			
					Independence			
Loss of habitation	Air pollution	Food and water damaged		Cultural Understanding				
	Animal Welfare		Animal Welfare	Community Project Goal				
					Environmental Considerations			
						Air pollution	Groundwater contamination	
							Environmental Considerations	Seismic activity

Building on from these community-specific factors for your community project, you can now begin to visualize in greater detail the impact of your community project through developing success criteria. Success criteria enable you to think through the impact of your community project at varying degrees of success.

You may also find it useful to create a simple Y-Chart that allows you to think about what your community project goal will look like, sound like and feel like for those who will be impacted.

ACTIVITY: Y-CHART

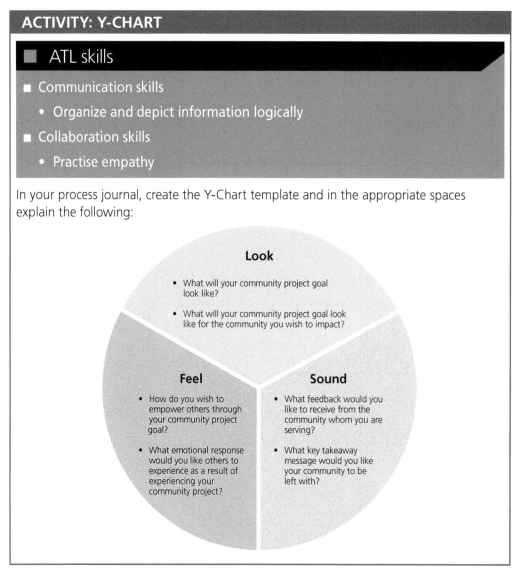

ATL skills

■ Communication skills
  • Organize and depict information logically
■ Collaboration skills
  • Practise empathy

In your process journal, create the Y-Chart template and in the appropriate spaces explain the following:

Look
• What will your community project goal look like?
• What will your community project goal look like for the community you wish to impact?

Feel
• How do you wish to empower others through your community project goal?
• What emotional response would you like others to experience as a result of experiencing your community project?

Sound
• What feedback would you like to receive from the community whom you are serving?
• What key takeaway message would you like your community to be left with?

The ideas presented in the Y-Chart and the Lotus Diagram together should provide a quality foundation for developing success criteria that ensures you are truly engaging in service as action that is thoughtful and appropriate.

Success criteria

Using your explanation for the community-specific factors of your community project and the impact you wish it to have, you can begin to logically think through just what will make your community project a success through developing success criteria. There are different approaches you can use to create success criteria. Three of these approaches are:

■ Pathways to Success
■ Target circles
■ Single-point rubric.

The success criteria you develop will be transferred to your proposal for action and is a way in which you can demonstrate how your proposal for action is appropriate and thoughtful.

■ Pathways to Success

Pathways to Success allows you to visualize and think deeply about the various pathways that will lead to you engaging successfully in service as action and ensuring you address the community-specific factors you have identified.

To develop your Pathways to Success, you need to think deeply about the important community-specific factors relevant to your community project. You will need to carefully consider what each important factor will look like at different degrees of success.

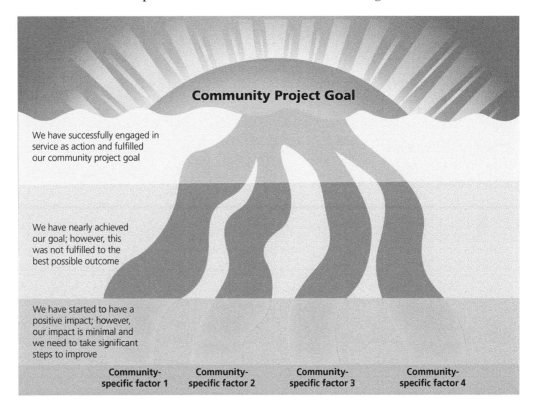

Community Project Goal

We have successfully engaged in service as action and fulfilled our community project goal

We have nearly achieved our goal; however, this was not fulfilled to the best possible outcome

We have started to have a positive impact; however, our impact is minimal and we need to take significant steps to improve

| Community-specific factor 1 | Community-specific factor 2 | Community-specific factor 3 | Community-specific factor 4 |

At the start of your journey to community project success, consider what just starting to have a positive impact will look like within the community-specific factors you have identified. Then, consider what nearly achieving your goal will look like within these community-specific factors. Finally, think about what successful engagement in these community-specific factors looks like, in order to engage successfully in service as action and fulfil your community project goal.

An example of the Pathways to Success for a highly challenging goal is as follows (this example is just focusing on one community-specific factor – language needs – however, you will find that you will have more than one factor to consider):

Community Project goal	
My community project goal is to create a Public Service Announcement (PSA) that advocates for the reversal of the new fracking policy, through education of the realities of fracking and providing the audience with options for how they can take action and join the anti-fracking advocacy movement.	
We have **successfully** engaged in service as action and fulfilled our community project goal	Our PSA shows the realities of fracking and provides our audience with options for how they can take action and join the anti-fracking advocacy movement. Finally, our PSA is communicated via primarily visual communication tools using images from thenounproject.com. To enhance the message of the visuals we have overlaid appropriate music and sound effects. Our communication is direct and clear so people from different languages can clearly understand what we are communicating and the direct impact of fracking on their current way of life. We have extracted all the necessary key points from our research and transferred these to provocative and clear messages.
We have **nearly** achieved our goal; however, this was not fulfilled to the best possible outcome	Our PSA shows the realities of fracking and provides our audience with options for how they can take action and join the anti-fracking advocacy movement. However, our PSA is mostly communicated via oral communication with both our faces being visible for half of the PSA. Our communication is still a bit too long and far too detailed using mostly written language with some visuals. We have extracted some key points from our research and transferred these to emotional messages, but they need more clarity.
We have **started** to have a positive impact; however, our impact is minimal and we need to take significant steps to improve	Our PSA shows the realities of fracking and provides our audience with options for how they can take action and join the anti-fracking advocacy movement. However, our PSA is primarily communicated via oral communication with both our faces being the primary things visible. Our communication is quite long and far too detailed using only written language. We have not extracted the key points from our research and transferred these to clear messages.
	Community-specific factor 1 We need to consider the language accommodations that our PSA will need to include as many individuals in our community are from diverse Indigenous communities and speak a variety of languages. English is often a third, fourth or fifth language for many of those we will be communicating to.

As you can see, at each progressive step the community project goal is being met, but without addressing the community-specific factors identified, the service as action is not as effective as it could be.

ACTIVITY: PATHWAYS TO SUCCESS

■ ATL skills

- ■ Critical-thinking skills
  - • Analyse complex concepts and projects into their constituent parts and synthesize them to create new understanding
  - • Identify obstacles and challenges
  - • Identify trends and forecast possibilities

- ■ Collaboration skills
  - • Take responsibility for one's own actions
  - • Practise empathy
- ■ Organization skills
  - • Set challenging and achievable goals

In your process journal, draw a Pathways to Success layout. Remember, you can add as many pathways (that is, community-specific factors) as necessary in order to develop a successful community project.

You should consider the questions below when thinking deeply about the community-specific factors you have identified. This will help you to develop a detailed, appropriate and thoughtful Pathways to Success.

We have successfully engaged in service as action and fulfilled our community project goal	• What is the best possible outcome for this community-specific factor? • What does success within this factor look like for the community you are serving? • How has carefully including this community-specific factor helped to achieve your community project goal?
We have nearly achieved our goal; however, this was not fulfilled to the best possible outcome	• What still needs to be addressed in seeking to develop a positive outcome within this community-specific factor? • What will nearly achieving your goal look like for the community you are serving? • What will you need to reflect on in order to go the next step and ensure this community-specific factor helps to fulfil your community project goal?
We have started to have a positive impact; however, our impact is minimal and we need to take significant steps to improve	• What does beginning to have a positive outcome look like for this community-specific factor? • What will you need to re-evaluate in order to successfully include this community-specific factor in your community project goal?

Target Circles

Another way you could develop your success criteria is by using Target Circles. Like the Pathways to Success, you need to think deeply about the important community-specific factors relevant to your community project, then consider what each important factor will look like at the different stages of reaching your target – your community project goal.

In the outer ring, consider what just starting to have a positive impact will look like within the community-specific factors you have identified. In the middle ring, consider what nearly achieving your goal will look like within these community-specific factors. Finally, think about what successful engagement in these community-specific factors looks like. At this point you have hit the target – you have successfully engaged in service as action *and* the identified community-specific factor has been addressed. For an example of the different degrees of success, see the example provided in the Pathways to Success.

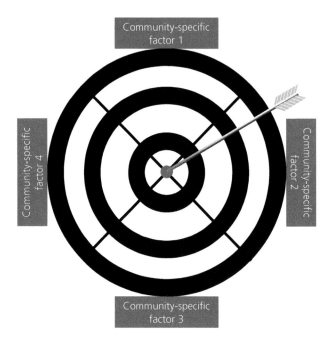

ACTIVITY: TARGET CIRCLES

■ ATL skills

■ Critical-thinking skills

- Analyse complex concepts and projects into their constituent parts and synthesize them to create new understanding
- Identify obstacles and challenges
- Identify trends and forecast possibilities

■ Collaboration skills

- Take responsibility for one's own actions
- Practise empathy

Either using a big piece of butcher paper and pens or in your process journal, draw up the Target Circles layout. Remember, you can add as many sections (i.e. community-specific factors) as necessary in order to develop a successful community project.

Consider the questions below when thinking deeply about the identified community-specific factors you will need to make when developing detailed, appropriate and thoughtful Target Circles:

We have successfully engaged in service as action and reached our target – our community project goal	• What is the best possible outcome for this community-specific factor? • What does success within this consideration look like for the community you are serving? • How has the need you are seeking to address within this community been successfully met through carefully including this community-specific factor?
We have nearly reached the target; however, this was not fulfilled to the best possible outcome	• What still needs to be addressed in seeking to develop a positive outcome within this community-specific factor? • What will nearly achieving your goal look like for the community you are serving? • What will you need to reflect on in order to ensure you can go that next step to ensure this community-specific factor is successfully included in fulfilling your community project goal?
We are on the target board; however, our impact is minimal and we need to take significant steps to improve	• What does beginning to have a positive outcome look like for this community-specific factor? • What will you need to re-evaluate in order to successfully include this community-specific factor in your community project goal?

Single-point rubric

Another way to ensure the important community-specific factors you have identified in order to successfully achieve your goal are met is by creating a single-point rubric. A single-point rubric only includes criteria for success at the successful level. The aim of the single-point rubric is to provide a structure for self-assessment, peer-assessment, mentor-assessment or supervisor-assessment to give targeted feedback on areas that need working on, as well as ways that you have exceeded your own expectations.

The single-point rubric is a simple layout, like this:

Areas for improvement	Success criteria	Exceeding expectations

In the centre column, explain how you will carefully address the community-specific factors you have identified. Your explanation can provide detail for how you will ensure that the community-specific factor you have selected is sufficiently met. Think of what this community-specific factor will look like, how it will make others feel, and the lasting impact you wish to leave with the community you are serving.

An example of a single-point rubric in action using the community project goal referred to in the Pathways to Success is as follows:

Areas for improvement	Success criteria	Exceeding expectations
In the opening scene, you have used a wind turbine symbol as the positive choice. Perhaps for our context, you could use a solar panel symbol as this is more common and accessible in our community.	Our PSA shows the realities of fracking and provides our audience with options for how they can take action and join the anti-fracking advocacy movement. Finally, our PSA is communicated via primarily visual communication tools using images from thenounproject.com. To enhance the message of the visuals we have overlaid appropriate music and sound effects. Our communication is direct and clear so people from different languages can clearly understand what we are communicating and the direct impact of fracking on their current way of life. We have extracted all the necessary key points from our research and transferred these to provocative and clear messages.	The use of visuals telling the story of fracking damage are well timed with the music and sound effects. The overall impact is powerful and very easy to understand regardless of language barriers.

As you begin your project and engage in service as action, choose strategic points throughout to seek feedback from the community you are serving, family, friends, mentors, your supervisor or any other person or group of people who can offer you accurate and targeted feedback. Giving and receiving meaningful feedback is an important part of successfully engaging in the community project.

The benefit of the single-point rubric for your planning is that you are not only planning for service as action, but also strategically planning for collaboration with others in order to receive meaningful feedback.

ACTIVITY: SINGLE-POINT RUBRIC

◼ ATL skills

- ◼ Critical-thinking skills
  - Analyse complex concepts and projects into their constituent parts and synthesize them to create new understanding
  - Identify obstacles and challenges

- Identify trends and forecast possibilities
- ◼ Collaboration skills
  - Take responsibility for one's own actions
  - Give and receive meaningful feedback

In your process journal, create a three-column table similar to the example below.

Areas for improvement	Success criteria	Exceeding expectations

Remember, the community project is about others. As you develop success criteria, practise empathy and take the time to think from the perspective of the community you are serving. Gather their feedback, their ideas, and their hopes and aspirations – this will help you to really connect with the community you are serving.

At this point in our Community Project Skills for Success book, we are going to pause developing a proposal for action. We will now move into creating a detailed and accurate plan and record of the development process of the community project.

At the end of this chapter, we will return to developing a detailed, appropriate and thoughtful proposal for action using our newly created organizational tools.

Plan and record the development process

Before you transfer your community-specific factors and success criteria into a proposal for action for your community project, it is a good idea to think ahead and plan. Draw together your investigation and success criteria into a detailed and accurate plan for how you intend to place your community project goal into action.

Planning for your community project requires you to carefully think about the following:

- ◼ The time frame you have to complete the community project.
- ◼ The resources you already have and the resources you will need.
- ◼ What skills you will need to develop in order to serve the need in the community you have chosen.

What you create in this section of your community project journey will need to be continually reflected on and most likely adjusted as you take action and serve the community you have chosen.

It is essential that you create an achievable plan for your community project. This requires you to think ahead and consider the time frame, resources and materials that you need in order to serve the need in the community.

There are several ways you can create and present a detailed and accurate plan and record of the development process of the project. When choosing one or several methods for planning and recording the development process of your community project, choose the method that suits you best.

■ Iceberg structure

To begin your brainstorming and to help your initial thinking of how you will create a detailed and accurate plan for your community project, you can use an iceberg structure.

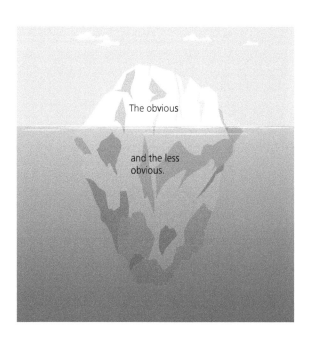

The top of the iceberg is the impact of your actual community project goal, the service as action the community you are serving will actually see and experience. The bottom of the iceberg is what only you will see and includes the hidden and behind-the-scenes parts of your community project.

An example of how you can use the iceberg structure for a highly challenging community project goal is below.

Community Project goal:

Through collaboration with members of the Autism Society, my community project goal is to create and publish a children's book that can educate my peers on just what autism is and how our school can become a more inclusive place. I will showcase this book at the school open day.

The top of the iceberg structure:

My peers will be presented with an informative and engaging children's book that clearly shows the facts about autism. They will have a foundational understanding of just what autism is, how autism affects people and how they can be inclusive and support those who have autism.

The bottom of the iceberg structure:

Communicate with key members of the Autism Society to gather first-hand information on what they most need to be communicated through my book.

Engage in research of the what and how of autism. Gather both primary and secondary sources of information of how myself and my peers can support and be inclusive of those who have autism.

Collaborate with my Language and Literature teacher to gather feedback on the most effective way to transfer information in a creative and engaging way for a children's book.

Contact an online publishing company and organize the publication and printing of my book.

Book a stall at the school open day to showcase my book.

As you can see from the example above, the iceberg structure is simply a tool to think about what goes unseen in actually putting your community project goal into action. This can begin your initial thinking of what you need to carefully plan for in order to successfully serve the community you have chosen to serve.

ACTIVITY: ICEBERG STRUCTURE

■ ATL skills

Critical-thinking skills

- Analyse complex concepts and projects into their constituent parts and synthesize them to create new understanding
- Identify obstacles and challenges

The obvious

and the less obvious.

In your process journal, create an iceberg template.

For the top of the iceberg, consider the following questions:

- What do you wish the end result of your community project goal to be?
- What impact do you wish to make on the community you are serving?
- What will be evident when you have met the need in the community you are serving?

Place your ideas at the top of the iceberg.

Now, fill in the bottom of your iceberg and consider the effort that needs to go into achieving your goal. Think about the following questions:

- What will be unseen and placed into action in the background?
- What will you need to create? What communication do you need to make?
- Which resources will you need and what support from others will you require?

Place your ideas for these considerations at the bottom of the iceberg.

■ Ishikawa

The Ishikawa scaffold is another method you can use to create a detailed and accurate plan for your community project. The Ishikawa enables you to think backwards from your community project goal to the support mechanisms you will need to achieve it. The Ishikawa uses the cause and effect principle: the causes, or the actions you take, generate an effect. The effect is the impact of your service as action when you place your community project goal into action. The Ishikawa scaffold allows you to be as detailed as you wish, it all depends on just how precise and detailed your 'fish bones' become.

There is another way in which you can create an Ishikawa to achieve your community project goal. You can sort the steps that you need to take in order to serve the need in the community you have chosen into categories such as: resources, time, organization and activities.

For example, in the **resources** category, you can outline the resources you need, such as a particular app, materials, finances, and so on.

In the **time** category, you can outline the time frame you have and how much time needs to be allotted to developing the various steps of your community project.

In the **organization** category, you can outline the various roles required to achieve your community project goal along with communication that needs to take place.

And finally, in the **activities** category, you can outline the various activities that need to occur in order for you to serve the need in the community you have chosen. An activity could be a flyer distribution via social media, using specific hashtags that will attract the right audience or an information evening to gather support for your project and raise awareness.

An example of the Ishikawa scaffold for a highly challenging community project goal using these categories is given below.

Community project goal: *My community project goal is to create an informational flyer that communicates the what, why and how of giving blood and will provide my school community with opportunities to participate through hosting a Blood Drive during student-led conference week.*

ACTIVITY: ISHIKAWA

■ ATL skills

■ Critical-thinking skills
- Analyse complex concepts and projects into their constituent parts and synthesize them to create new understanding
- Use models and simulations to explore complex systems and issues

■ Creative-thinking skills
- Apply existing knowledge to generate new processes

■ Transfer skills
- Combine knowledge, understanding and skills to create solutions

Create a 'fish skeleton' Ishikawa in your process journal, similar to the example below.

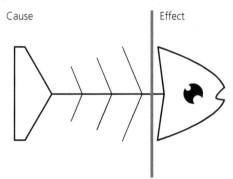

At the head of the Ishikawa – the effect – place a brief summary of your community project goal. Imagine

you are at the end point of your community project and you have successfully addressed the need in the community you have chosen. Ask yourself the following questions:

■ What will I need to have achieved in order to reach this endpoint?
■ What order will I need to place each step in, so I can achieve this goal?
■ What support and resources will I need to employ?
■ How will I begin to put this goal into action?

Create as many skeletal structures, or causes, that you need in order to achieve your goal. Along the skeleton describe what you will achieve and when in order to serve the need in your community.

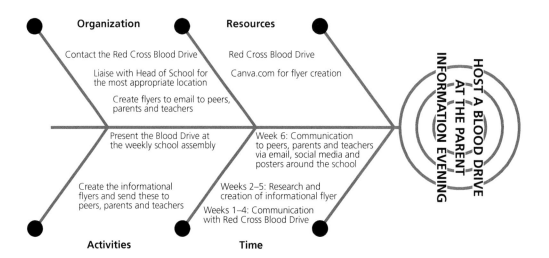

Gantt chart

Another approach to planning and recording the development process of your community project is through creating a Gantt chart. Put simply, a Gantt chart is a useful way to plan for a large project.

ACTIVITY: GANTT CHART

ATL skills

- Organization skills
  - Plan short- and long-term assignments
  - Meet deadlines
  - Set goals that are challenging and realistic
- Collaboration skills
  - Take responsibility for one's own actions

Using a processing program, create a table similar to the example opposite:

Simply place in the left-hand column all the steps, in logical and time-bound order, that need to be completed in order to place your community project goal into action and address the need in the community you have chosen. Then, along the top, place your time frame. You can use school weeks or specific dates – the choice is up to you.

Colour in the correct spaces for the time frame in which you wish to achieve this goal. You can change the colour once you have completed this step or make notations if you are unable to keep to the time frame and explain the reasons why.

Your Gantt chart is a way that you can forward plan, a way to gather a big picture of what needs to be achieved within the allocated time frame as outlined in your proposal for action, and it is also flexible to help you adjust your planning based on possible interruptions and setbacks.

Objective	Resources	Week 10	Week 1	Week 2	Week 3	Week 1	Week 2	Week 3	Week 4	Week 5	Week 6	Week 7	Week 8	Week 9	Week 10
Investigation:															
Define community project goal	Seqta – Learn and individual devices	▓													
Define research			▓												
Research process	Primary and secondary sources			▓											
Evaluation of sources					▓										
Planning:															
Assign roles for completion							▓								
Create rubric for success							▓								
Refine Gantt chart							▓								
Taking action:															
Capture photographs	iPhones, individual devices, transport, internet connection, Instagram Text-Write and Tumblr apps.								▓						
Create quotes and hashtags									▓	▓					
Record progress in process journal										▓					
Edit images and synthesize										▓					
Double-check and get group feedback											▓				
Publish on Tumblr												▓			
Reflecting:															
Evaluate against rubric for success	Seqta – Learn and individual devices												▓		
Write TEDx-style talk script														▓	
Create Appendix and Bibliography													▓		
Double-check, edit and refine													▓		
Presenting:															
Deliver TEDx-style talk for report	Projector, individual devices, recording device														▓

■ Kanban board

Another approach you can take to planning and recording the development process of your community project is through creating a Kanban board. Like the Gantt chart, this is a useful way to plan for a large project.

The Kanban board is a great approach if you are working in pairs or as a group of three. This is a way to ensure the roles and responsibilities are equally distributed and also a visualization tool to ensure each group member is on track and completing the necessary tasks to effectively achieve your community project goal.

ACTIVITY: KANBAN BOARD

▪ ATL skills

- ▪ Organization skills
  - • Plan short- and long-term assignments
  - • Meet deadlines
  - • Set goals that are challenging and realistic
- ▪ Collaboration skills
  - • Take responsibility for one's own actions

A Kanban board helps you plan for and organize progress by simply visualizing what needs to be done; it shows what is 'in progress' and what 'has been accomplished'. Use sticky notes on paper, a whiteboard or you can utilize one of the many digital software packages available to create a Kanban board.

In the 'To do' column prioritize what needs to be achieved. Once you have this task in motion, move it to the 'Doing' column. When you have completed this task, move it to the 'Done' column.

You will find that as more and more of your tasks are met you can visualize the 'Done' column of your Kanban board growing. So, when the going gets a bit tough and perhaps motivation and time management are becoming a bit tricky, this will give you the incentive to keep going and keep moving towards achieving your community project goal.

Make the most of a blend of analogue and digital. You may choose to allocate a section of a wall at home to a large-scale Kanban board where you can track your progress. This is also a way of including your family and friends – and maybe even the community you are serving – as they can monitor your progress and celebrate your achievements with you.

To do	Doing	Done

▪ Scrum board

The Scrum board is also an approach you can choose to take in planning and recording the development process of your community project.

ACTIVITY: SCRUM BOARD

▪ ATL skills

- ▪ Organization skills
  - • Plan short- and long-term assignments
  - • Meet deadlines
  - • Set goals that are challenging and realistic
- ▪ Collaboration skills
  - • Take responsibility for one's own actions
  - • Give and receive meaningful feedback
- ▪ Reflection skills
  - • Consider personal learning strategies – what can I do to become a more efficient and effective learner?
  - • Demonstrate flexibility in the selection and use of learning strategies

The Scrum board is similar to the Kanban board, but is more descriptive and broken down into smaller chunks. Read through the following explanation and if this approach to planning suits you, you can then create your own Scrum board.

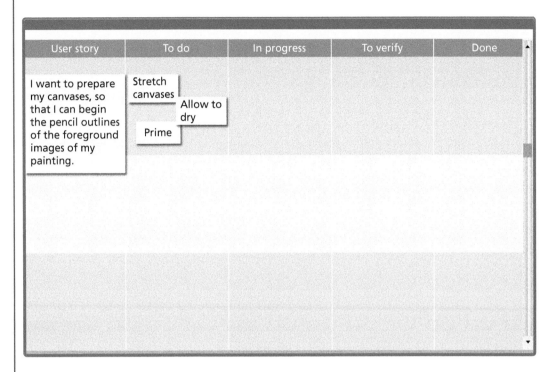

User story

The first column begins with what is called the 'User story'. This is simply a statement explaining the 'what' and 'why' of each of the steps of your community project. Each User story can be created using the following sentence prompts:

- I want to ... so that I can ...

To do

The second column is where you simply bullet point what needs to be done in order to achieve the goal of your User story.

In progress

The third column is where you move your To do sticky note or text box to the 'In progress' column. If you have come across challenges, jot these down. Going back to your To do list, add what you need to do in order to overcome this challenge. This is a fluid board that visualizes your process based on both your setbacks and your progress.

To verify

The fourth column is where you verify your progress. This is a strategic and intentional point to self-assess your progress against your success criteria. Using your rigorous criteria for success (that should be continuously referred to throughout the process) self-assess what you have achieved thus far to ensure that you are aiming for the best possible outcome of your community project. Seek feedback from your supervisor, peers, mentor, family and friends. If you are not happy with your self-assessment, head back to your User story or To do list and think about what needs to be adjusted in order for you to improve. Repeat as necessary.

Done

Finally, the fifth and last column is where you move your To do sticky note or text box to visualize process success. Give yourself a pat on the back, high-five those close by or post via social media the successful completion of one of your User stories!

Develop a proposal for action to serve the need in the community (continued)

Now that you have thought deeply about the various community-specific factors to address in your community project, have identified a plan for community project success and considered the time and resources you need to engage in service as action, you can now draw these together to create a **proposal for action**.

A proposal for action is simply a representation of your careful considerations and your detailed and accurate plan to place your community project goal into action. It is based on the community-specific factors you have carefully thought through and your strategic planning for implementing your community project.

There are several ways that you can present your proposal for action. Select the approach that best suits your community project goal and unique approach to learning. Remember, these approaches and scaffolds can be modified to suit your needs. Feel free to change, add and take away elements according to your own and your community project needs.

The first step to creating a proposal for action is to ensure that you have the information required to develop your proposal. This should include the following:

1 The community you are serving.

2 The need you are serving within this community.

3 How you plan to engage in service as action, and what type of service you will engage in.

4 The global context your community project is best aligned with.

5 How you know you will have successfully implemented service as action – your success criteria that outlines how you have considered the community-specific factors.

6 The time and resources you have organized in order to place your community project goal into action.

■ Expanding circles

One of the approaches you can take to creating your detailed, thoughtful and appropriate proposal for action is through Expanding circles. Expanding circles allow you to represent your proposal for action while at the same time showing the incremental process you have undertaken to reach this point in your community project.

ACTIVITY: EXPANDING CIRCLES

■ ATL skills

■ Communication skills

- Use appropriate forms of writing for different purposes and audiences

■ Collaboration skills

- Take responsibility for one's own actions

■ Organization skills

- Set goals that are challenging and realistic
- Plan strategies and take action to achieve goals

Create the following scaffold in your process journal. Remember, you can modify this according to your needs.

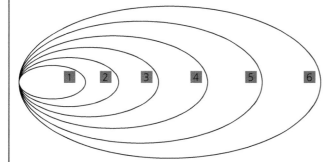

1 In the central circle, place the community you are serving.

2 In the second circle, place the need within the community you will be serving.

3 In the third circle, place how you plan to engage in service as action, and what type of service you will engage in.

4 In the fourth circle, place the global context your community project is best aligned with.

5 In the fifth circle, place how you know you will have successfully implemented service as action.

6 In the sixth circle, place the time and resources you have organized in order to place your community project goal into action.

Remember to employ your visual literacy skills and use both written and visual text to communicate your proposal for action. Identifying and selecting visual tools and icons is another way in which you can organize your ideas and strengthen your communication skills.

■ Action Brief

Another approach you can take to creating your detailed, thoughtful and appropriate proposal for action is through an Action Brief. An Action Brief is very similar to the Design Brief you will be accustomed to creating in your MYP Design subjects. An Action Brief allows you to represent your proposal for action in a concise and cohesive written form that presents the information required in your proposal for action.

ACTIVITY: ACTION BRIEF

■ ATL skills

■ Communication skills

- Use appropriate forms of writing for different purposes and audiences

■ Collaboration skills

- Take responsibility for one's own actions

■ Organization skills

- Set goals that are challenging and realistic
- Plan strategies and take action to achieve goals

In your process journal, employ your written communication skills and create a heading entitled 'Action Brief'. Refer to the six information steps in the Expanding circles activity to create your brief.

Be direct and straight to the point! There is also a variety of software and online sites that you can use to place your Action Brief into an infographic and creatively communicate your concise proposal for action.

■ Letter

Another way in which you can create a detailed, thoughtful and appropriate proposal for action is through a letter to the community you are serving or a representative of this community. If you are engaging in research or indirect service, and are unable to make direct contact, address this letter to your supervisor. A letter is simply a way to present your proposal for action and share your proposal for action with key individuals who can offer feedback and encouragement.

ACTIVITY: LETTER

■ ATL skills

- Communication skills
  - Use appropriate forms of writing for different purposes and audiences
- Collaboration skills
  - Take responsibility for one's own actions
- Organization skills
  - Set goals that are challenging and realistic
  - Plan strategies and take action to achieve goals

In your process journal, compose a draft of your letter to either the community you are serving, a representative of this community or your supervisor. Remember to ensure your letter is written in such a way as to engage the reader – if necessary use persuasive language conventions to support your communication.

Remember to ensure your letter includes the six-step information above to demonstrate how your proposal for action is detailed, thoughtful and appropriate.

Send your letter to the identified recipients and remember a successful community project involves both giving and receiving meaningful feedback. Take any feedback given from the recipient on board and critically and creatively think about how you can absorb this feedback and make any necessary improvements.

There are many other ways in which you can present your detailed, thoughtful and appropriate proposal for action. Draw on the various communication skills you have and use these to communicate your proposal for action. For example, if you enjoy drawing create a comic strip proposal for action; if you enjoy filmmaking create your proposal for action in a short film format; if you enjoy typography and design consider how you can employ your skills to present your proposal for action. There are so many communication possibilities; remember to take risks and make the community project your own, drawing on your passion and strengths.

Demonstrate self-management skills

This part of the community project journey is embedded throughout each stage of the project.

Self-management skills are ways of organizing the actual project as well as organizing your state of mind.

In your process journal, ensure you document and make very visible the ways in which you have organized the community project, as well as the ways in which you have organized your state of mind. Remember to include examples and scenarios in order to make sure your thinking is visible.

Organization skills include:

- meeting deadlines
- sticking to your goals
- making plans that are logically and sequentially efficient
- maintaining your process journal with regular updates
- selecting and using technology effectively and productively.

Through developing rigorous community-specific factors success criteria, a detailed, thoughtful and appropriate proposal for action, and planning and recording the process of your community project, you will have the support mechanisms in place to meet deadlines that are logically and sequentially organized for optimal efficiency and to help you stick to your goals, all the while maintaining your process journal with regular updates. Remember to take risks and be open-minded to the variety of technology within your reach. Select and use technology in an effective and productive manner that is best suited to the needs of your project.

Affective skills include:

- Mindfulness – practise strategies to overcome distractions and maintain mental focus.

Mindfulness strategies empower you to focus your mental and physical energy on to a certain aspect of your community project in such a way that you are not easily distracted by external distractors and can maintain mental focus.

As MYP students you have busy academic schedules. Currently, you are engaged in eight different subject areas that each have assessment schedules and quite possibly also homework to balance as well. Along with this you also have active social lives, both online and offline. When practising mindfulness strategies to overcome distractions and maintain mental focus, it is good to consider how you orientate yourself in both place and time.

ACTIVITY: MAINTAINING MENTAL FOCUS

ATL skills

- **Affective skills**
  - Mindfulness – practise strategies to overcome distractions and maintain mental focus

Place: Set aside a location that has minimal distractions in order for you to intentionally position yourself in a location that supports you maintaining mental focus. Turn off your notifications. Unplug from social media. Actively organize yourself and your community project resources in such a way that you can maintain mental focus. If you are working as a group on your community project, select a communal place such as the school library, an empty classroom or a member of your group's home.

Time: Refer consistently to the planning schedule that you have developed; be conscious of creating the time for a balanced approach to effective community project completion. The entirety of the community project should take around 15 hours to complete, make the most of each minute of these hours. Choose your best time of the day for optimal concentration and mental focus.

Perseverance: Demonstrate persistence and perseverance and help others demonstrate persistence and perseverance. This begins with a growth mindset. A growth mindset requires that we are optimistic, and we have the tools to challenge faulty thinking when the project becomes challenging.

Throughout the duration of your project, you will undoubtedly come across points where you will need to persist and persevere. A learner with a growth mindset does not give up at this point; they simply stop, pause and reflect in order to reassess how to move forward from there.

ACTIVITY: THE MOSCOW METHOD

■ ATL skills

- Organization skills
  - Plan short- and long-term assignments
  - Meet deadlines
- Affective skills
  - Perseverance
  - Self-motivation
  - Resilience

An effective way of reassessing your progress and making decisive steps forward is to employ the MoSCoW method. Break down what you need to achieve into smaller chunks and break this down into what you 'must do' and 'should do' to achieve this goal, 'could do' to go over and above, and 'won't do' to ensure optimal persistence and perseverance.

Must do	Jot down what is absolutely essential for you to persevere and persist to achieve this goal and serve the community you have chosen.
Should do	Jot down what you should do to persevere and persist to achieve this goal.
Could do	Jot down what you could do to ensure you are working towards self-assessing your service as action at an excellent level, even though you may be struggling to persist and persevere.
Won't do	Intentionally plan for blocking out distractions and hindrances to your persevering and persisting to complete this goal

Seeing these small successes will help you to persist and persevere. Remember, community project success is made up from multiple small successes that culminate into significant project success.

Self-motivation: Practise analysing and attributing causes for failure, and practise positive thinking.

Self-motivation requires habits of mind that focus on thinking about the big picture. At the beginning of the community project, you will have established your goal by explaining why this project is important to you and why your goal is important to the community you are serving. When problems occur, and you experience setbacks, it is a good idea to reflect back on why your project is important to you. And of most importance, reflect on just why this service as action is important to the community you are serving.

When attributing causes for setbacks or failure, it is important to keep the positives in mind. It is a good idea to begin with listing what has gone well so far and then exploring from there the causes for these setbacks and failure. Once you have analysed and attributed the causes for failure, ensure you then refocus on the bigger picture of why persevering and persisting in this project is important to you and the community you are serving.

When we experience setbacks and failure in a large project it can be easy to go down a negative spiral of doubt, practising positive thinking can help build the growth mindset required for community project success.

Reflection skills include:

■ being open-minded, developing new skills, techniques and strategies for effective learning

■ keeping a journal to record reflections

■ taking note of how your thinking is changing by using the 'I used to think ...' 'Now I think ...' sentence prompts

■ being principled by identifying strengths and weaknesses of personal learning strategies (self-assessment)

■ taking risks by trying new learning strategies and reflecting on the effectiveness of this new learning strategy.

EXPERT TIP

Be kind to yourself, give yourself the space to breathe and reflect. This kindness to oneself and space for reflection will support you in creating the best possible community project and, in turn, will effectively meet the need that you seek to address in the community you have chosen.

Due to the sustained project-based nature of the community project, it is beneficial to stop and pause at points along the way and reassess your progress, celebrate what you have achieved thus far and clarify the steps forward that you will take.

ACTIVITY: COMPASS POINTS

ATL skills

■ Collaboration skills
  • Take responsibility for one's own actions
  • Give and receive meaningful feedback

■ Reflection skills
  • Consider personal learning strategies
  • Demonstrate flexibility in the selection and use of learning strategies

The Compass Points visible thinking routine is an effective tool to calibrate your community project situation and assess 'where to go from here'. You may have already used this in your earlier planning stages.

E = Excitements: What excites you about what you have achieved so far?
W = Worries: What have you found worrisome about your project progress so far?
N = Needs: What else do you need to find out, or skills do you need to acquire, to move forward?
S = Steps or Suggestions: What should your next step be?

Show your peers, a representative from the community you are serving, family or supervisor your Excitements, Worries and Needs – what suggestions do they have for you?

Information gathered from your reflections may mean you need to adjust your planning and even your proposal for action; this is fine, remember, the community project is a journey of continual reflection. In your process journal, make sure you document your reflection of your organization and self-management skills.

EXPERT TIP

Be honest – managing our state of mind is often one of the trickiest skills to develop. The more we reflect on our ability to organize ourselves and work on the best ways to manage our state of mind, the more we help ourselves and others.

Supervisor Check-in

- Share your planning with your supervisor. Your supervisor may be able to support you by organizing strategic check-in points at crucial points as you take action.
- Show your supervisor your proposal for action and ensure they have given you feedback, and you have taken this feedback on board.
- Share your process journal with your supervisor. Let them see the progress of your community project thus far.
- Discuss with your supervisor how you are doing with your self-management affective skills. Your supervisor could have ideas to share with you that can support you learn to develop these skills.

A great tool to use when considering how you can communicate your community project planning process is through a SERVE conversation. You could have this prepared and ready for your meeting with your supervisor and use this as a flow for how you will discuss your project thus far.

Strategic: Demonstrate to your supervisor how you have strategized and planned for a successful community project.

- *How have you strategically planned for successfully placing your community project goal into action? What next steps will you take?*

Empathy: Demonstrate how you have strengthened your empathy skills and how you can continue to strengthen your empathy skills.

- *How have your empathy skills been strengthened so far? How can your community project goal enable you to strengthen your empathy skills? As you take action, how can your community project empower others to strengthen their empathy skills?*

Realistic: Demonstrate to your supervisor how your community project goal is realistic.

- *How can your community project goal become a reality? What can the community you are serving expect to experience as a result of your service?*

Viable: Demonstrate how you have carefully thought through how viable your community project goal is and how you have carefully considered the community-specific factors to ensure successful service as action.

- *What community-specific factors have you considered? How have you thought deeply and strategically about these in order to ensure your service as action is thoughtful and appropriate?*

Excellent: Demonstrate how you are striving for both personal and academic excellence through the community project.

- *How are you taking risks and striving to be an excellent learner through the community project? What Learner Profile attributes have you developed and how can you provide examples of this?*

CHAPTER SUMMARY KEY POINTS

- The second objective of the community project is planning.

- To develop a thoughtful, detailed and appropriate proposal for action you need to take into account community-specific factors that could impact your ability to effectively serve the community you have chosen. You could use the following methods:
  - Lotus diagram
  - Y-chart.

- To demonstrate detail and thoughtfulness you can create success criteria that show how you will ensure the community-specific factors you need to make will enhance the impact of your community project. You could use the following methods:
  - Pathways to success
  - Target circles
  - Single-point rubric.

- It is a good idea to develop a plan and process for just how you will place your community project goal into action prior to developing your proposal for action. You could use the following methods:
  - Iceberg structure
  - Ishikawa
  - Gantt chart
  - Kanban board
  - Scrum board.

- Continuously develop and reflect on your ability to demonstrate self-management skills, managing both the project and your state of mind. Self-management skills include:
  - Organization
  - Reflection
  - Affective skills.

- Affective skills are often the trickiest skills to develop. The key to success here is to be vulnerable, seek help when you need it, and remember to keep persevering.

Taking action

Taking action is where you apply your thinking, communication and social skills to creating your community project product/outcome. Make sure you consistently reflect and document your reflections in your process journal – make the process of creating visible.

Don't forget your global context! Take time to reflect on how your understanding of your chosen global context is deepening as a result of putting your investigating and planning into action.

Demonstrate your creative-thinking skills, critical-thinking skills and transfer-thinking skills. You can employ the various visible thinking routines in this chapter to help you communicate your thinking skills.

Demonstrate your communication and social skills. Questions and guidelines in this chapter can help you articulate how you have demonstrated your communication and social skills.

Taking action

■ ATL skills	
■ Communication skills	■ Critical-thinking skills
■ Collaboration skills	■ Creative-thinking skills
■ Organization skills	■ Transfer skills
■ Affective skills	■ Reflection skills

LEARNER PROFILE ATTRIBUTES	
Inquirer	Caring
Thinker	Risk-taker
Communicator	Balanced
Principled	Reflective

At this stage in the community project, you have:

■ defined a goal to address a need within a community based on personal interest

■ identified prior learning and subject-specific knowledge and explained how this can be transferred to your project and serve as a foundation for research and transfer

■ started to engage in research and demonstrated how you are a principled learner by practising academic honesty

■ developed a proposal for action to serve the need in the community

■ started planning and recording the development process of the project

■ demonstrated self-management skills.

Demonstrate service as action as a result of the project

Now it's time for the *doing* part of your community project, where you pull together all of the investigating and planning that you have engaged in and take action to carry out service in your chosen community. As you place your goal into action make sure you document your service through photographs and/or video clips, interviews with your fellow group members or with members of the community that you are serving. You will need this evidence of action for your presentation, and it will provide valuable material to support reflection.

ACTIVITY: REFLECTING ON AFFECTIVE SKILLS

ATL skills

- Communication skills
  - Negotiate ideas and knowledge with peers and teachers
- Collaboration skills
  - Encourage others to contribute
- Reflection skills
  - Consider ATL skills development (What can I already do? How can I share my skills to help peers who need more practice? What will I work on next?)
  - Keep a journal to record reflections

Engaging in service as action requires you to demonstrate certain affective skills, which are those skills related to feelings or emotions. With a partner (another student, someone from your group or from another group), consider which of these skills you demonstrated while taking action in your project. Give concrete examples of how you demonstrated those skills. Be sure to record your thoughts in your process journal as well.

Different types of affective skills include:

Mindfulness
- Practise focus and concentration
- Practise strategies to develop mental quiet
- Practise strategies to overcome distractions

Perseverance
- Demonstrate persistence and perseverance
- Practise delaying gratification

Emotional management
- Practise strategies to overcome impulsiveness and anger
- Practise strategies to prevent and eliminate bullying
- Practise strategies to reduce anxiety
- Practise being aware of body–mind connections

Self-motivation
- Practise analysing and attributing causes for failure
- Practise managing self-talk
- Practise positive thinking

Resilience
- Practise 'bouncing back' after adversity, mistakes and failures
- Practise 'failing well'
- Practise dealing with disappointment and unmet expectations
- Practise dealing with change

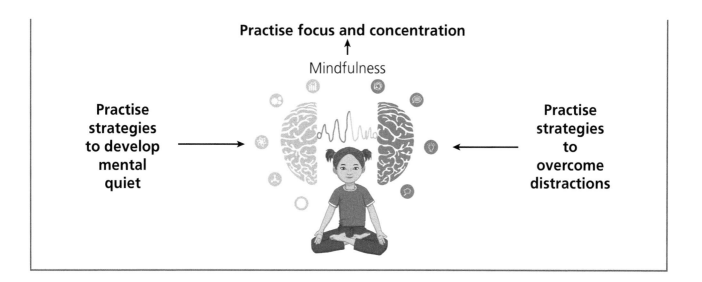

Demonstrate thinking skills

Throughout the community project, you will have demonstrated different types of thinking. In the context of the approaches to learning, these are:

- Critical-thinking skills
- Creative-thinking skills (sometimes referred to as innovation)
- Transfer skills.

Remember to be explicit about your thinking skills and make your thinking visible within your process journal; many of the activities in this book will have guided you towards this approach.

> **EXPERT TIP**
>
> If you haven't already done so, it is a good idea to go back and label your process journal entries with the different ATL skills that are demonstrated, including the thinking skills listed above. This 'signposting' will help your supervisor identify these skills when it comes to assessing your project and will also make it easier for you to reflect on how and when you have developed these skills throughout the project.

Critical-thinking skills that you can employ as you place your community project goal into action involve analysing and evaluating issues and ideas. You will find that you need to critically think through developing solutions to obstacles that you encounter, evaluating your progress and making informed decisions on the next steps of your community project. Critical-thinking skills will also be evident as you consider the service as action experience from the perspective of the community you are serving and using the information gathered through this consideration to make informed, empathetic and ethical decisions.

Creative-thinking skills involve generating new ideas and considering new perspectives. Creative-thinking skills necessary for you to successfully take action and meet the need in the community you have chosen, include considering different alternatives and making unexpected connections. As you make progress and place your goal into action you may find that you develop a new and better way to address the need you are serving. Through brainstorming and designing improvements to your community project you will be exploring different alternatives to successful service as action. Remember, just like a community is diverse and ever changing, likewise, your community project can evolve as you progress.

Transfer skills enable you to use skills and knowledge from one area of expertise or subject to effectively take action and place your community project goal into action. In Chapter 3 you have identified the prior learning and subject-specific knowledge relevant to your community project. As you take action, it is important to demonstrate how this knowledge and prior learning is consistently relevant to your project. No doubt you have taken a risk and the very nature of your goal is highly challenging, therefore there will be unfamiliar elements in your community project goal. Your challenge in developing and strengthening your transfer approaches to learning skills is to effectively transfer these familiar skills and knowledge into the unfamiliar elements of your community project.

As you implement your proposal for action and place your community project goal into action, you need to make your thinking visible in your process journal. Ensure you reflect continuously and show how you are developing your critical-thinking, creative-thinking and skills.

To support you in the process of critically and creatively thinking and transferring these skills into your proposal for action, the following strategies can work as a guide for your thinking and transfer skills.

ACTIVITY: CLAIM – SUPPORT – QUESTION

ATL skills

- Critical-thinking skills
  - Practise observing carefully in order to recognize problems
  - Revise understanding based on new information and evidence

How is your understanding of the community you have chosen developing? How is your understanding of the need in the community you are addressing developing?

To explain and provide evidence of how your understanding of the community and need is developing, you can employ the visible thinking routine **Claim – Support – Question**. This routine enables you to explain clearly what you have learned, provides evidence and continues the inquiry process through asking further questions.

- Make a **claim** about the community and/or the need. A claim is an explanation or interpretation of some aspect of what is being examined.
- Identify **support** or evidence for your claim. What do you now know? What new knowledge do you have? How can you provide evidence to support this claim?
- Raise a **question** related to your claim. What may make you doubt the claim? What seems unresolved? What isn't fully explained? What further ideas or issues does your claim raise?

ACTIVITY: PROBLEM-SOLVING

■ ATL skills

- ■ Critical-thinking skills
  - Practise observing carefully in order to recognize problems
  - Propose and evaluate a variety of solutions
- ■ Creative-thinking skills
  - Create novel solutions to authentic problems

What obstacles have you encountered?

As you progress through the process of implementing service as action, record in your process journal obstacles that you encounter. Putting a goal and plan into action comes with its challenges, so be sure to think carefully about how you can overcome these obstacles.

How have you overcome obstacles through problem-solving?

Describe and explain how you have overcome the obstacles you have encountered in the taking action process. Take photographs, screenshots, recordings, sketches and any other evidence to support your problem-solving skills.

ACTIVITY: NEW IDEAS AND PERSPECTIVES

■ ATL skills

- ■ Critical-thinking skills
  - Analyse complex concepts and projects into their constituent parts and synthesize them to create new understanding
- ■ Creative-thinking skills
  - Consider multiple alternatives, including those that might be unlikely or impossible
- ■ Transfer skills
  - Apply skills and knowledge in unfamiliar situations
  - Transfer current knowledge to learning of new technologies

How have you generated creative ideas and considered new perspectives? How have you made connections between what you already knew and what you are learning through taking action?

Generating novel ideas often comes as a result of exploring others' ideas, thinking deeply and challenging our own thoughts and ideas, and building on these ideas as a result. A visible thinking routine that you can employ is **Connect – Extend – Challenge**.

As you take actions and put your ideas and skills acquired through investigating and planning into practice, ask yourself the following questions:

- ■ How are the ideas and information **connected** to what I already knew?
- ■ What new ideas did I get that **extended** or broadened my thinking in new directions?
- ■ What **challenges** or puzzles have arisen from the ideas and information presented?

ACTIVITY: FEEDBACK

■ ATL skills

■ Critical-thinking skills

- Revise understanding based on new information and evidence

- Propose and evaluate a variety of solutions

■ Creative-thinking skills

- Practise flexible thinking – develop multiple opposing, contradictory and complementary arguments

■ Transfer skills

- Combine knowledge, understanding and skills to create products or solutions

How have you taken feedback on board and incorporated this into achieving your community project goal?

Giving and receiving feedback is an important skill throughout the process of taking action. The quality of the feedback given and received can determine the overall quality of your service as action. The skill of giving and receiving feedback often lies in the questions we ask to dig deeper and broaden the scope of feedback. A concise visible thinking routine that you can employ is the *What Makes You Say That? (WMYST?)* routine.

As you receive feedback, dig deeper by asking the question *WMYST?* as many times as necessary in order to gather the best possible depth of feedback. In turn, as you give feedback, share this visible thinking routine with the person or group of people you are giving feedback to, so that they can receive the best possible depth of feedback from you.

ACTIVITY: FLEXIBLE THINKING SKILLS

■ ATL skills

■ Critical-thinking skills

- Consider ideas from multiple perspectives

- Analyse complex concepts and projects into their constituent parts and synthesize them to create new understanding

■ Creative-thinking skills

- Make unexpected or unusual connections between objects and/or ideas

- Practise flexible thinking – develop multiple opposing, contradictory and complementary arguments

- Practise visible thinking strategies and techniques

■ Transfer skills

- Combine knowledge, understanding and skills to create products or solutions

How have you developed flexible thinking strategies surrounding the ethical impact of your community project?

Using the following visible thinking routine, Circle of viewpoints, develop your flexible thinking strategies to consider the personal and ethical impact of your service as action on your chosen community.

■ I am thinking of *[your service as action]* from the point of view of …

■ I think … *[describe the personal and ethical impact of your service as action from your chosen viewpoint of a member of the community you are serving. Be an actor – take on the character of your viewpoint]*. Because … *[explain your reasoning]*

■ A question/concern I have from this viewpoint is …

ACTIVITY: USING YOUR PRIOR KNOWLEDGE

■ ATL skills

- Critical-thinking skills
  - Revise understanding based on new information and evidence
- Creative-thinking skills
  - Make unexpected or unusual connections between objects and/or ideas
- Transfer skills
  - Apply skills and knowledge in unfamiliar situations
  - Combine knowledge, understanding and skills to create products or solutions

How have you employed your prior learning as you have participated in service as action?

Scroll or flick through your process journal to find where you have outlined the prior learning that will be employed to place your community project goal into action. Provide evidence and explain how you have employed this prior learning effectively to meet the need in the community you have chosen.

How have you used your subject-specific knowledge and skills in multiple contexts?

Scroll or flick through your process journal to find where you have outlined the subject-specific knowledge that will be employed to place your community project goal into action. Provide evidence and explain how you have employed this subject-specific knowledge effectively to meet the need in the community you have chosen.

ACTIVITY: GLOBAL CONTEXT INSIGHT

■ ATL skills

- Critical-thinking skills
  - Revise understanding based on new information and evidence
- Creative-thinking skills
  - Consider multiple alternatives, including those that might be unlikely or impossible
  - Make unexpected or unusual connections between objects and/or ideas
- Transfer skills
  - Combine knowledge, understanding and skills to create products or solutions

What new insight do you have into your chosen global context?

Using the following thinking routine, *I used to think … but now I think …* , reflect on how your thinking has changed as a result of new insights into your chosen global context.

Use these sentence starters to explain your deeper insight into your chosen global context:

I used to think … but now I think … and this is why …

The global contexts are very broad and complex for your project. Another way of explaining new insights into your chosen global context is through creating an iceberg structure to show a depth of understanding.

Draw an iceberg structure (as pictured opposite) and at the top of the iceberg, the part above water, jot down what you notice and what is obvious about the global context you have chosen through the lens of your community project. In the larger part under the water, dive deeper to examine the less obvious and explain the influences, values, beliefs and reasons for what you notice or what is obvious in the top part of the iceberg.

Make sure your responses to these questions are documented throughout your process journal. You may choose to spend some time responding to these questions or your own questions at one point in the project, or you may find that simply responding as you go works best for you. Draw pictures, jot down inspirational quotes, create diagrams, glue in printed images and articles – make your thinking as visible as possible.

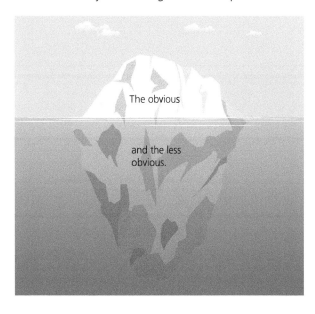

The obvious

and the less obvious.

Demonstrate communication and social skills

Engaging in service as action will also have required you to use and strengthen your communication and social skills.

Communication skills include verbal and non-verbal communication and listening. They can be demonstrated through interaction or through language. In the context of the community project, you will most likely have demonstrated your ability to communicate through interaction: you will have communicated with your peers if you worked on the project as a group, communicated with your supervisor, and no doubt communicated in some way with members of the community that you are serving.

You will also have demonstrated a range of social skills by collaborating with a variety of individuals, including your supervisor, throughout the course of your community project.

This part of the community project inquiry cycle is embedded throughout each step of the project. As you place into action your community project goal, you will be developing your communication and social skills. Ensure you reflect continuously and show how you are developing as both a collaborative learner and as a communicator.

How have you developed a deeper sense of empathy?

Through overcoming obstacles and solving problems, can you explain how you can understand and share the feelings that others have experienced when they have had to overcome obstacles and solve problems?

How have you developed intercultural understanding?

Have there been instances in your service as action journey where you have learned to understand and value cultures, belief systems and languages other than your own?

Can you explain how this development of intercultural understanding has enabled you to have a deeper understanding of your own culture(s), belief systems and language(s)?

ACTIVITY: RESOLVING CONFLICT

■ ATL skills

- ■ Communication skills
  - Give and receive meaningful feedback
  - Negotiate ideas and knowledge with peers and teachers
- ■ Collaboration skills
  - Take responsibility for one's own actions
  - Listen actively to other perspectives and ideas
  - Encourage others to contribute

How have you managed to resolve conflict and work collaboratively with others?

Throughout sustained projects that require collaboration and communication skills, conflicts can arise and create a need for employing conflict resolution skills. This can especially happen if you are engaging in the community project with a partner or in a group of three. An approach to effective conflict resolution that you are no doubt familiar with as IB students is through creating essential agreements.

When creating an essential agreement with the person or group of people you are collaborating with, it is beneficial to use the following steps as a guide:

1 Realign yourselves with the purpose: Why have you chosen to serve this community? Why is it important that you meet the need you have identified within this community?

2 Consider what helps you and the person or group of people you are collaborating with to best produce the work required. Think about the environment, physical structures and preferred learning styles.

3 Discuss what this looks like, sounds like and feels like. You can create a Y-chart to record your discussion.

4 Using the information from this discussion, create *We will ...* statements. For example, *We will listen actively to one another and wait until the other person has finished sharing their ideas before responding.*

5 As you progress in the collaborative process, refer to your essential agreement should conflict arise and you need a reminder of the agreed-upon approaches to collaboration and communication.

How have you taken responsibility for your actions?

Reflect on the process of taking action and fulfilling your community project goal. Where have you had to take responsibility for your actions? Perhaps you overspent your budget, or struggled to manage your time effectively and needed to reassess how you will go further, or perhaps you have experienced a setback in the process of taking action? Reflect on how you have been a principled learner who has owned what has happened rather than blaming others, and how by employing your self-management skills you have moved forward.

How have you encouraged others to contribute to your community project? How have you worked effectively with members of the community you are serving? How have you worked effectively with your supervisor and taken their ideas on board?

Think of how you have engaged with members of the community, experts and your community project supervisor. How have you encouraged them to contribute to your community project? How have you sought meaningful feedback from others as a means of them contributing to your community project?

How have you exercised leadership?

As a self-managed and independent student, you have leadership over your community project journey that requires coordination, collaboration and communication with others. Exercising leadership requires a clear goal and communication and negotiation skills. How have you communicated the needs of your project through exercising leadership to help you achieve your community project goal? Reflect on how your leadership skills have developed and how these developing skills will support you in further studies and project management.

ACTIVITY: GIVING AND RECEIVING FEEDBACK

■ ATL skills

- **Communication skills**
  - Give and receive meaningful feedback
  - Make inferences and draw conclusions
- **Collaboration skills**
  - Listen actively to other perspectives and ideas
  - Encourage others to contribute

How have you given and received meaningful feedback?

If you have employed the visible thinking routine *What Makes You Say That? (WMYST?)* or a similar approach, how have you further developed skills for giving and receiving meaningful feedback? Another means of giving and receiving meaningful feedback is through employing the Ladder of Feedback.

1 Begin at the first rung of the ladder and start by offering or receiving meaningful feedback through **clarification** of the focus of your community project. You can ask and encourage others to ask you the following questions:
   - I wasn't sure about...?
   - Could you help me better understand...?

2 Follow this by moving to the second rung (figuratively), discussing the **value** of this part of your community project. You can use the following sentence starters as a guide:
   - What I like is …
   - One opposite point is …

3 Then move to the third rung and express **concerns** surrounding this part of your community project. You can use the following sentence starters as a guide:
   - Have you considered …
   - What I wonder about is …
   - Perhaps you have thought about this, but …

4 Moving to the final rung of the feedback ladder you can offer **suggestions** and seek suggestions from others. The following sentence starter can be employed as a guide:
   - Can I suggest that …

How have you organized and depicted information logically?

Take some time to reflect on how you are presenting the record of your development through your community project journey in your process journal. It is a good idea to highlight sections according to the community project objectives. For example, when you are problem-solving by employing your critical- and creative-thinking skills, highlight in your process journal how this is you demonstrating your ATL thinking skills. This organization and logical depiction of information will help others understand your community project journey and also provides support at the end of this project when you are writing your community project report, piecing together your presentation and presenting your process journal extracts for submission.

Make sure your responses to the questions above that you believe are relevant to your process of taking action, are documented throughout your process journal. You may choose to spend some time responding to these questions or your own questions at one point in the project, or you may find that simply responding as you go works best for you.

One of the central ATL skills that you will develop through the community project is the skill of empathy. It is through communication, collaboration and deep thinking that our empathy grows and is increasingly strengthened. As you meet the identified need in the community you have chosen, it is a good idea to pause at critical steps along the way as you take action and consider the reasons for the perspectives towards your project. An effective tool for unpacking and strengthening your empathy skills is the visible thinking routine Step Inside.

ACTIVITY: STEP INSIDE

ATL skills

- Collaboration skills
  - Practise empathy
- Creative-thinking skills
  - Analyse situations from different perspectives

Identify a member of the community you are serving. Using the following questions as your guide, consider just what they know, feel and believe to be true about the impact of your community project on their community.

1 What can the person or thing perceive?

2 What might the person or thing know about or believe?

3 What might the person or thing care about?

Using the ideas you have gathered from this routine, consider the impact this has on just how you take action and implement your community project goal. This approach is also useful for when you encounter setbacks and perhaps even resistance at various points in community project implementation.

EXPERT TIP

Like with thinking skills, it is advisable to signpost those process journal entries which explicitly demonstrate your development of communication and social skills.

Supervisor Check-in

- Share the evidence of your service as action with your supervisor. You need someone to help you celebrate your successes – and perhaps reflect on the challenges you may have faced.
- Show your supervisor your process journal entries. Try to articulate how you have demonstrated the various thinking skills throughout your project and point out where this thinking is visible in your journal.
- Discuss the experience of working with others to achieve a goal – both the positive and negative aspects.

CHAPTER SUMMARY KEY POINTS

- The 'taking action' stage of the project is the culmination of all of your investigating and planning. It is the *doing* part of the project.

- Engaging in your service as action activity will allow you to demonstrate certain affective skills such as mindfulness, perseverance, emotional management, self-motivation and resilience.

- You will need to make visible evidence of critical and creative thinking and transfer in order to demonstrate thinking skills.

- Your community project will also have given you an opportunity to demonstrate communication and social skills. You may use the questions and guidelines in this chapter to help you.

- Evidence of the development of each of these skills should be clearly signposted in your process journal.

- You will develop empathy skills during your community project through communication, collaboration and deep thinking.

Reflecting

Action

Reflect on how well you achieved your desired outcome. Is there anything you would like to change?

Inquiry

Reflect on your inquiry. Which of the learner profiles are you demonstrating? How well are you integrating your chosen global context?

Reflecting

Reflection is a key part of the inquiry cycle, and should be repeated throughout your project.

Reflecting

■ ATL skills	
■ Communication skills	■ Affective skills
■ Self-management skills	■ Transfer skills
■ Thinking skills	■ Collaboration skills
■ Reflection skills	

LEARNER PROFILE ATTRIBUTES	
Inquirer	Principled
Communicator	Reflective

At this stage in the community project, you have:

■ defined a goal to address a need within a community based on personal interest

■ identified prior learning and subject-specific knowledge relevant to the project and have explained how this can be transferred to your project and serve as a foundation for research

■ engaged in research and demonstrated how you are a principled learner by practising academic honesty

■ developed a proposal for action to serve the need in the community

■ started planning and recording the development process of the project

■ demonstrated self-management skills

■ demonstrated service as action as a result of the project

■ demonstrated thinking, communication and social skills.

So that's a wrap, right? Your community project is complete!

Well, not exactly. If the experience ended here, just after the taking action stage, you would be missing out on valuable opportunities for more meaningful learning. The American philosopher, psychologist and educational reformer John Dewey famously stated, 'We do not learn from experience … we learn from reflecting on experience.' The service as action project is not the endgame; thoughtful, honest reflection on what you have learned from the experience is the ultimate goal.

Reflection is not something that happens just at the end of the community project; it is part of the whole process. As an IB learner, reflection is at the heart of everything you do. Indeed, reflection is a key component of the inquiry cycle, and this cycle can – and should – be repeated multiple times throughout the project. In order to demonstrate your best work, you will need to make your reflections obvious. That means that you should show evidence of ongoing reflection in your process journal. You should also reflect explicitly on the three strands of Criterion D in your presentation.

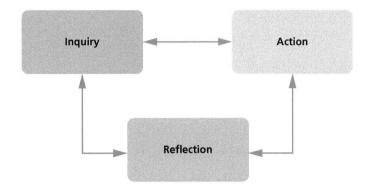

■ Evaluate the quality of the service as action against the proposal

As you pull all of your reflection together, the first step in formally presenting your reflection is to evaluate the quality of the service as action against the proposal. This means thinking back to the planning stages and considering to what extent you achieved the criteria you set out for yourself.

EXPERT TIP

It is very likely that your project will undergo some form of change between the proposal and the taking action stage. Making changes should not be viewed as a failure of your proposal; this evolution is part of the process. As long as you reflect meaningfully on why you have made these changes, then you can still demonstrate success against the assessment criteria. Equally, even if the service as action has 'failed', that does not necessarily mean that your community project has failed; you can still demonstrate valuable learning through failure.

ACTIVITY: EVALUATING SUCCESS

■ ATL skills

- Affective skills
  - Self-motivation:
    - Practise analysing and attributing causes for failure
  - Resilience:
    - Practise 'bouncing back' after adversity, mistakes and failures
    - Practise 'failing well'
    - Practise dealing with disappointment and unmet expectations
    - Practise dealing with change
- Reflection skills
  - Identify the strengths and weaknesses of personal learning strategies (self-assessment)

Look back at the success criteria for the community-specific factors you established during the planning

stage (Chapter 4). You may have developed Pathways to Success, Target Circles, Single-point Rubric or any other approach to developing strategies and success criteria.

Thinking objectively, answer the following questions:

- How well did you meet your criteria? What evidence can you provide to demonstrate the level of success that you feel you have achieved?
- If you failed in a particular area, why might that be? (Hint: Consider your own role in that failure; try not to make excuses or put blame onto others.)
- What would you do differently if you could complete your service as action again? How could the project be improved?
- What has been the impact of your project on the community that you served? For this reflection to be meaningful (and credible), ask a member of that community for their feedback.

Don't confuse your own criteria for the service as action with the overall assessment criteria for the community project.

■ Reflect on how completing the project has extended your knowledge and understanding of service learning

The next stage of reflection requires you to consider how your knowledge and understanding of service learning has developed throughout the course of the project. Service learning is essentially learning about a community in order to serve this community to the best of your ability. Perhaps you came to the project with very little understanding of what service learning is; maybe you thought there was no connection between service and learning. Or perhaps you thought you already had a good knowledge of what service learning is all about but as you engaged in your project you uncovered new layers of understanding. As you reflect on this aspect of the project, you will need to be specific about how completing the project has extended your knowledge and understanding of service learning. At what stage(s) did your perspective change?

ACTIVITY: SERVICE LEARNING – I USED TO THINK … BUT NOW I THINK …

■ ATL skills

■ Reflection skills

- Consider content (What have I learned about service learning? What don't I yet understand? What questions do I now have?)

■ Critical-thinking skills

- Recognize unstated assumptions and bias

- Revise understanding based on new information and evidence

Consider what you knew or thought about service learning before engaging in your community project versus what you know or think now. If you held certain assumptions or biases before the project, consider where those assumptions or biases came from. Why did you think a certain way? If you changed your mind about any aspect of service learning, why was that? What (or who) influenced you on your journey towards new understanding? Complete the chart below based on your reflections.

I used to think …	But now I think …

When you have completed this activity individually, share your ideas with a partner – either from your group or from another group. How did their reflection compare with yours? Did anything they shared with you lead to new knowledge or even greater understanding of service learning? If so, be sure to record that in your process journal.

In order to thoroughly evaluate service learning, it is a good idea to reflect on the experience itself, of placing your community project goal into action and meeting the need in the community you have chosen to serve. An approach to reflecting on the experience of service learning is through a modified Kolb's Experiential Cycle. This has been modified to suit the the purposes of community project reflection.

ACTIVITY: EXPERIENCE REFLECTION CYCLE

■ ATL skills

■ Reflection skills

• Consider personal learning strategies

– What can I do to become a more efficient and effective learner?

■ Transfer skills

• Making conclusions

The modified Kolb's Experiential Cycle can guide you through the cycle of reflecting on:

1 your community project goal and the key knowledge and understanding you needed in order to serve the community effectively

2 the actual experience and how this knowledge and understanding impacted your service

3 conclusions you draw from the experience and the need to learn about a community in order to serve effectively

4 how this experience will inform your future service learning.

Your community project goal and the key knowledge and understanding you needed in order to serve the community effectively

How this experience will inform your future service learning

The actual experience and how this knowledge and understanding impacted your service

Conclusions you draw from the experience and the need to learn about a community in order to serve effectively

In your process journal, draw the cycle and use it to reflect on the actual experience of service learning. Remember, service learning is essentially learning about a community in order to serve this community to the best of your ability.

■ Personal reflection

Now that you have engaged in an in-depth service learning experience through completing the community project, you can take the time to reflect personally on your growth as an individual.

Through service, you will often find that your thoughts, feelings and motives are transformed in a very positive way. You will also often find that you are much more caring and thoughtful of others as you have had to think deeply about the needs of others and respond to those needs.

ACTIVITY: PERSONAL REFLECTION

■ ATL skills

■ Critical-thinking skills

• Draw reasonable conclusions

Take time to quietly reflect on how you have personally grown – be honest and celebrate who you are becoming as a caring citizen. In your process journal, use the following scaffold to consider the different ways you may have grown.

Saying	Thinking	Being
• What changes do you notice to how you speak to and about others?	• How have you thought differently? What do you wonder about yourself as a learner?	• Have you changed? Have you become more patient? More respectful?
Doing	**Having**	**Feeling**
• Have you done something that you normally would not do? • Have you helped in a way that you had not thought you were capable of?	• Do you have more of something? More knowledge? Respect? Compassion? Determination?	• Have you felt different? Empathized? Inspired? Worried? Admired?

◼ Reflect on your development of ATL skills

Throughout the community project, you will have developed several of the approaches to learning skills. At various stages of the process, you will have had the opportunity to demonstrate communication, social, self-management, research and thinking skills. You will need to reflect explicitly on how you have developed and demonstrated these different skills in your community project presentation, with reference to specific evidence that demonstrates your development as an IB learner.

The community project has many benefits. You have the opportunity to serve a community and meet the needs of others: this is one of the most important features of our shared humanity. Another benefit is that you have the opportunity to master key approaches to learning skills and by doing so become a more thoughtful and self-managed learner.

As you reflect on your development of skills throughout the community project, consider how you have advanced along the continuum of skill mastery:

1	2	3	4
Novice – I am beginning to learn a new approach to learning skill	**Learner** – I am developing this new approach to learning skill	**Practitioner** – I am confidently and effectively using this new skill	**Expert** – I can accurately use this skill and share this skill with others

It is likely that you have already transitioned forward in this continuum through all the learning experiences in your MYP subjects. It is important to continuously seek to improve your approaches to learning skills so you can be more independent as a learner and also support others through sharing what you have learned.

> **EXPERT TIP**
>
> If you have labelled your process journal entries according to which ATL skills are best demonstrated, then it will be much easier to present specific evidence of your skills development.

ACTIVITY: IN THE HOT SEAT – REFLECTING ON ATL SKILLS DEVELOPMENT

◼ ATL skills

- Collaboration skills
  - Encourage others to contribute
  - Listen actively to other perspectives and ideas
- Reflection skills
  - Consider ATL skills development (What can I already do? How can I share my skills to help peers who need more practice? What will I work on next?)

Use the following questions to interview a peer. When performing the role of interviewer, don't be afraid to probe your partner for specific examples or evidence to support their answers. As they respond, record their reflections and give them your notes when you have finished. Sometimes having someone else write down your ideas can help you view them more objectively.

When you have finished interviewing your partner, switch roles so that you're in the hot seat. Articulating your ideas orally is good practice for presenting your community project to a larger audience.

Communication skills

Investigating: This part of the community project inquiry cycle requires lots of listening and taking information on board – how have your listening skills developed?

Planning: Through your primary and secondary source research, has your ability to share your ideas with others and listen to their ideas improved?

Taking action: As you put your proposal for action into action, how have you developed your ability to communicate with others in a positive way?

Reflecting: Overall, how have you developed as an effective communicator?

Social skills

Investigating: How have you grown in confidence by interacting with primary and secondary sources?

Planning: How have you developed as a collaborative learner? What are the strengths of working with other people? What are the limitations of working with others?

Taking action: How has your ability to collaborate with others improved?

Reflecting: Collaboration requires maturity – how have you matured as a learner through collaboration?

Self-management skills

Investigating: Through your investigation, have you become a more compassionate person?

Planning: How have your organization skills improved?

Taking action: How have you been able to develop the way in which you manage your emotions? Are you more resilient?

Reflecting: How have you developed as a reflective learner?

Research skills

Investigating: How have you developed as a researcher? How has your ability to find and analyse information improved?

Planning: How have you been able to transfer your research and source analysis skills to planning for service?

Taking action: How has your ability to use technology and social media grown as you have put your investigating and planning into action?

Reflecting: How has your ability to find, interpret, judge and create information improved?

Thinking skills

Investigating: How have your critical-thinking skills developed? Do you have more skills to use to help you analyse and evaluate information?

Planning: How have your creative-thinking skills developed? Are you able to come up with new ideas and consider issues from different points of view?

Taking action: How have your transfer skills developed? How has your ability to transfer primary and secondary research, classroom learning and prior learning to your proposal for action developed your transfer skills?

Reflecting: How have you become a deeper thinker? How have you learned to take time to think deeply about an issue?

If you have enough students to form groups of three, you can appoint one person to the task of note-taker, who can also evaluate the quality of the responses using the table below. As the note-taker/evaluator, be sure to justify your evaluation and provide some suggestions for how your peer can improve their reflection.

Question	Response	Quality of response				Notes
		Excellent	Good	Fair	Poor	

EXPERT TIP

The assessment criteria do not specifically ask you to reflect on how you have demonstrated certain Learner Profile traits; however, the Learner Profile is implicitly woven through each of these strands. For example, you may have demonstrated risk-taking when making changes to your proposal. You may have demonstrated open-mindedness when reflecting on how your understanding of service learning has changed. And you will most certainly have demonstrated the ability to be reflective! Making reference to the Learner Profile might be a nice addition to your presentation – and a stepping stone towards the type of reflection you will do individually as you continue through your school experience and beyond.

Supervisor check-in

- Share your reflections on an ongoing basis with your supervisor. Celebrate successes, discuss challenges you have faced and how you have overcome them, and reflect on what you have learned from the project and how you can apply that learning to new situations.
- Evaluate the success of your project with your supervisor. Your supervisor may be the one who is ultimately giving you your grade, but it is worth noting that assessment is not something that is done *to* you; you should be a part of the assessment process by evaluating your own work and reflecting on the feedback that your supervisor has given you.
- Show your supervisor your process journal entries and explain which ATL skills are demonstrated (and how) in each entry.

CHAPTER SUMMARY KEY POINTS

- Reflection is not a linear process. It is part of the inquiry cycle and will form part of all stages of the project.

- You should show evidence of ongoing reflection within your process journal and presentation.

- There are three specific aspects of reflection that you will need to explicitly address in the 'Reflecting' section of your presentation:
  - Evaluating the quality of the service as action against the proposal.
  - Reflecting on how completing the project has extended your knowledge and understanding of service learning.
  - Reflecting on your development of ATL skills.

Presenting the Community Project

Format

- The community project presentation is an oral presentation presented to an audience.
  The presentation is a formal reflection of the process of engaging in the community project.

Structure

- Presentation organized around the community project objectives.

Academic honesty

- Academic honesty must be practised throughout the process, and all sources must be acknowledged according to recognized conventions.
- You will be required to submit an academic honesty form. This form will need to be signed by your supervisor to authenticate your work.

Process Journal extracts

- Depending on the organization of your community project you will need to include process journal extracts to support the information in your presentation.

Presenting the Community Project

At the end of your community project, you must present your project. There are multiple ways in which you can choose to present, however the requirements are that your presentation is oral and delivered to an audience. Your audience may include your peers, the community you have served, your supervisor, your family and friends or the larger community. The audience will vary based on the organization of your school and how your supervisors and Projects Coordinator have decided to structure the community project presentations. There may perhaps even be a student council that gathers your feedback on how you wish to present your community project and this student body may coordinate this with the relevant school leaders.

To support you in planning for your community project presentation, this chapter is organized in sequential order. The order of this chapter is as follows:

1 **Time frames**

   ■ the time frames permitted for your community project presentation.

2 **Content**

   ■ what to include in your community project presentation.

3 **Format and preparation**

   ■ choosing a format for how you wish to creatively present your community project and support for preparing your presentation.

4 **Visual aids**

   ■ tips for how to enhance your presentation through visual aids.

5 **Self-assessment and rehearsing your presentation**

   ■ questions to consider for self-assessment of your community project presentation and an encouragement to rehearse.

6 Submission

- what to submit to your supervisor or school Projects Coordinator when you present your community project presentation.

Time frames

To provide you with a time frame scope for your community project presentation, consider the following and identify which category you fall into:

- For an individual student presentation, the time allocated is **6–10 minutes.**
- For a group presentation, the time allocated is **10–14 minutes.**

If you have chosen to complete the community project in a group you will present as a group, but each group member should have the opportunity to speak during the presentation. Make sure you equally distribute the presentation roles among the members of your group.

Content

The content of your presentation will be the substance of what you will be sharing.

Before we move into the possibilities of how to approach the content of your presentation, let's begin with looking at what you can include in your community project presentation.

The IBO requirement for the content of your presentation is that the information you present is structured following the community project objectives. Your community project presentation must, therefore, include the following:

- Investigating
- Planning
- Taking action
- Reflecting

The following table is a breakdown of just what you can include in each section of the community project objectives. The ideas below come directly from each objective strand. These should all be evident in your process journal as you have documented your journey of service as action through achieving your community project goal. (If you are working in a pair or a group, remember to substitute 'I' for 'we'.)

Within the **Investigating** section of your community project presentation you can include the following:

An introduction to the community you are serving and the need you have addressed within this community. The clear and highly challenging goal you have chosen and how this is based on your personal interests.
Guiding questions: • How can I clearly communicate the need within this community that I have chosen to address? • How can I communicate the global context I have chosen for this project and why that context helps others understand just how important my community project goal is? • How can I communicate how this goal is based on personal interest? What evidence can I provide to support why this is of personal interest to me? Can I employ an anecdote to communicate how this community project goal is based on personal interest?
The prior learning and subject-specific knowledge that you have identified that has been consistently highly relevant to reaching your community project goal.
Guiding questions: • How can I communicate the prior learning I have transferred to my community project? • How can I communicate the subject-specific knowledge I have transferred to my community project? • How can I provide examples and explanations of how this prior learning and subject-specific knowledge has been consistently used throughout the community project?
An explanation of how you have demonstrated excellent research skills, both primary and secondary, to learn about the community you have served in order to address the need you have identified within this community.
Guiding questions: • How can I communicate the research skills I had at the start of the community project and how I have improved and broadened my research skills as a result of seeking to achieve my community project goal? • How can I communicate the types of research I engaged in throughout the community project? • How can I communicate how I practised academic honesty and thus developed as a principled learner?

Within the **Planning** section of your community project presentation you can include the following:

An explanation of how you have developed a detailed, appropriate and thoughtful proposal for action to serve the need in the community.
Guiding questions: • How can I communicate my detailed, appropriate and thoughtful proposal for action? • How can I communicate the community-specific factors I have considered in order to develop this detailed, appropriate and thoughtful proposal for action?
A description of how you have presented a detailed and accurate plan and record of the development process of the project.
Guiding questions: • How can I communicate the process of the community project so my audience understands just what went into implementing service as action? • How can I communicate the planning tools I chose to ensure successful service as action? • How can I communicate the thinking process of planning for this project and how I followed the plan I established? • How can I justify and explain the adjustments that I made to my plan?
Examples with explanations of how you have demonstrated excellent self-management skills.
Guiding questions: • How can I communicate my organization skills and how these have improved throughout the process of the community project? • How can I communicate how I have been mindful and how I have overcome distractions in order to remain mentally focused? • How can I communicate my reflection skills and how these have improved throughout the process of the community project?

Within the **Taking action** section of your community project presentation you can include the following:

Examples with explanations of how you have demonstrated excellent service as action as a result of the project – how you have placed your community project goal into action.
Guiding questions:
• How can I communicate just what I have achieved through placing my community project goal into action?
• How can I communicate the experience of service as action?
• How can I communicate the impact I have had on the community I am serving?
• How can I communicate how I addressed the need I have chosen within the community I am serving?
Examples with explanations of how you have demonstrated excellent thinking skills.
Guiding questions:
• How can I communicate the ways in which I have demonstrated critical-thinking skills? How can I communicate how my critical-thinking skills have improved through the process of the community project?
• How can I communicate the ways in which I have demonstrated creative-thinking skills? How can I communicate how my creative-thinking skills have improved through the process of the community project?
• How can I communicate the ways in which I have demonstrated transfer skills? How can I communicate how my transfer skills have improved through the process of the community project?
Examples with explanations of how you have demonstrated excellent communication and social skills.
Guiding questions:
• How can I communicate the ways in which I have demonstrated communication skills? How can I share how my communication skills have improved through the process of the community project?
• How can I communicate the ways in which I have demonstrated collaboration skills? How can I communicate how my collaboration skills have improved through the process of the community project?

Within the **Reflecting** section of your community project presentation you can include the following:

An explanation of how you have thoroughly evaluated the quality of the service as action against the proposal for action you developed in Chapter 4.
Guiding questions: <ul><li>How can I communicate how I have thoroughly evaluated the quality of the service as action I have implemented against the proposal for action I developed?</li><li>How can I communicate the effectiveness of the service as action I have implemented?</li><li>How can I communicate just how the global context I have chosen is evident throughout my community project?</li></ul>
Provide excellent reflections on how completing the project has extended your knowledge and understanding of service learning.
Guiding questions: <ul><li>How can I communicate my reflections on how my knowledge and understanding of learning about a community in order to serve them has been extended?</li><li>What new insight and ideas can I communicate about service learning?</li><li>What further questions do I have about service learning?</li></ul>
Reflection and explanation on how you have developed approaches to learning skills.
Guiding questions: <ul><li>How can I communicate how I have developed communication approaches to learning skills?</li><li>How can I communicate how I have developed research approaches to learning skills?</li><li>How can I communicate how I have developed self-management approaches to learning skills?</li><li>How can I communicate how I have developed social approaches to learning skills?</li><li>How can I communicate how I have developed thinking approaches to learning skills?</li><li>Most importantly, how can I share the ways in which I can support my peers develop ATL skills?</li></ul>

Format

The next step in your community project presentation process is to decide on a format. There are multiple options for how you can communicate your community project presentation. Consider your strengths, consider the resources you have available and consider how you can best communicate to the audience who will be informed of your community project journey.

This chapter provides just three possibilities for effective community project presentation. Your community project supervisor, Projects Coordinator and other members of your school will no doubt have a repertoire of other approaches to community project presentation. Be sure to employ your communication and social skills and ensure you have the correct information from your school in order to develop your community project presentation.

▨ Presentation format 1: Empowering narrative

The key to a successful community project presentation is to empower your audience through sharing not only the service as action you have implemented but also the process. Your goal is to inspire your audience to understand just how important your community project goal is, through communicating just how you have sought to meet the need in the community you have chosen.

Nancy Duarte, a well-known author and authority on presentations, in her TED Talk, *The secret structure of great talks*, shares the shape of a great presentation that captures just how effective communicators share their ideas and seek to inspire their audience. (This Talk and others can be found by searching 'teen' on www.ted.com/tedx or at www.ted.com.) This shape can be applied to your community project presentation to help you communicate clearly, effectively, and in such a way to inspire and empower your audience.

The idea of this shape is that you take your audience on a journey from the reality – the low point – to how you have improved both the community you are serving and your own approaches to learning skills. This shape allows you to capture your audience by developing a narrative of how you have positively impacted the community through meeting a need and how you have improved as an effective learner.

Here is an example of how you can use this shape to form your community project presentation. This example focuses on explaining improved communication ATL skills.

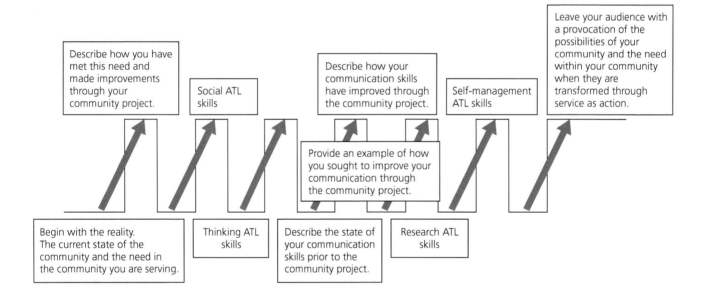

Highly challenging community project goal:

My community project goal is to create a partnership between my school and the Wildlife Park with the purpose of creating easy communication for my peers to report injured wildlife on their way to and from school. Through developing a location-based app, my peers can efficiently and accurately report injured wildlife to Wildlife Park Rangers, making the process of rescuing wildlife more timely and efficient.

Reality – this is where the ATL skill was at the beginning of the community project.

At the beginning of the community project, I struggled with presenting information in front of a live audience. The night prior to delivering an Individuals and Societies presentation I was feeling quite sick at the thought of standing up in front of my class and communicating my ideas. I knew that in order to effectively put my community project goal into action, I needed to improve my communication skills so I could effectively communicate with a live audience.

Moving upwards – this is how you sought to improve this ATL skill throughout the community project.

To improve my communication skills, I decided to focus on thorough preparation in order to improve my confidence in communicating and connecting with others. I organized the key information that I needed to present to the Wildlife Park into an information flyer that addressed the SWIH of my community project. This flyer also included a visual representation of the app I was developing. I then placed into bullet point order the key points of my communication with the Wildlife Park representative. These points were then transferred to palm cards using sticky notes attached to cardboard and I rehearsed my presentation. I then decided to practise delivering my presentation, so I contacted my community project supervisor and organized a time to meet in order to rehearse my presentation. I was then able to take the feedback given by my supervisor on board and adjust my palm cards.

The positive result – how my skills have improved throughout the community project.

I was successfully able to communicate to the Wildlife Park representative, and although I was nervous, I was well prepared and organized, therefore my nerves were calmed, and my confidence levels were increased. Now I have a process and personal approach to communicating information and communicating to a live audience that I can employ for future presentations. As I developed practical approaches to communicating, I can share this process with classmates to support my peers who, like me, have experienced great anxiety when it comes to communicating with a live audience.

As you can see from the example, the presentation begins with the reality of where an ATL skill was at the beginning of the community project, an explanation of how the skill was improved, and a reflection on the positive result.

Through your honesty and transparency in communicating your development as a learner and your development as a caring and empathetic citizen, you will empower your audience to reflect on themselves as lifelong learners and as caring and empathetic citizens.

ACTIVITY: EMPOWERING NARRATIVE

To begin planning for this style of community project presentation, it is a good idea to have a piece of butcher paper and a pen. Jotting down your ideas around this scaffold is a great way to organize your presentation.

Draw the shape below in the centre of your piece of paper.

At the beginning of your presentation, you can begin with the reality, explaining the need in the community and why the need exists. This is the starting point of your presentation. Then take your audience on a journey explaining how you met the need in this community and the positive impact you have made. This is the finishing point of this part of your presentation.

Then move into explaining the state of your ATL skills at the start of the community project, how you improved your ATL skills through placing your community project goal into action, and finish with their improved state and how you can support your peers through sharing these newly mastered skills.

To conclude your presentation, you can describe the community as it could be and then develop a call to action in order to inspire and empower your audience.

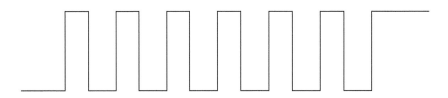

Presentation format 2: Golden Circles

Another approach to delivering an effective community project presentation is through the use of what is often referred to as the Golden Circles. The Golden Circles are a way in which you can communicate your community project journey beginning with the 'Why', setting up from the very beginning just how important your community project goal is. You can then take your audience on a journey into the 'How', the process of how you placed your important community project goal into action. Your presentation can then move into leading your audience on a journey into the 'What', what you have achieved and how you have met the 'Why' of your community project.

The Golden Circles are an effective way to capture your audience and ensure that your presentation clearly communicates the importance of your community project goal. The Golden Circles are also an effective way to introduce the community you have chosen and the need you have identified in this community in order to inspire empathy and a further call to action.

ACTIVITY: GOLDEN CIRCLES

To begin planning for this style of community project presentation, it is a good idea to have a piece of butcher paper and a pen. Jotting down your ideas around this scaffold is a great way to organize your presentation. Another option is to jot your ideas on sticky notes and place them in the appropriate places on the scaffold. This means you can move your ideas around as they further develop.

Draw the following shape in the centre of your piece of paper.

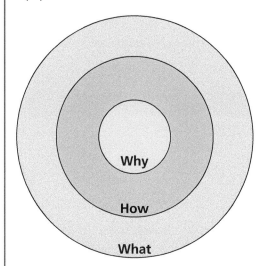

Why

In the centre – the 'Why' – you can creatively communicate the following:

- The community you are serving and why.
- The need in the community you have identified and why.
- Your community project goal and why.
- The global context you have chosen and why.
- Your proposal for action.

Make sure you communicate these key points of your community project through the lens of **why** your community project is important. Always think of the **why**. Place yourself in the shoes of your audience and consider how they can be influenced to understand just why your community project goal is important.

How

In the second ring – the 'How' – you can talk about the process. In this section you can include the following:

- The community-specific factors you have considered to ensure that you have indeed engaged in thoughtful and appropriate service as action.
- Your plan for placing your community project goal into action.
- How you have employed **self-management** ATL skills to meet the need in the community you have chosen and how these skills have improved through the process of the community project.
- How you have employed **social** ATL skills to meet the need in the community you have chosen and how these skills have improved through the process of the community project.

- How you have employed **research** ATL skills to meet the need in the community you have chosen and how these skills have improved through the process of the community project.
- How you have employed **thinking** ATL skills to meet the need in the community you have chosen and how these skills have improved through the process of the community project.
- How you have employed **communication** ATL skills to meet the need in the community you have chosen and how these skills have improved through the process of the community project.
- A reflection on the process of how you placed your community project goal into action. You can include:
  - anecdotes
  - 'I used to think … but now I think …' visible thinking routines.

Remember, this part of the Golden Circles is about the process. Be clear in communicating how you placed your community project goal into action. Refer to the beginning section of this chapter where the content of what goes into your community project presentation is explained. Make sure you address the guiding questions.

What

This final part of your community project presentation is about the impact. What impact have you had? What positive changes have occurred as a result of your service as action? What developments have you made as a learner? The focus here is on impact. In this section you can include the following:

- How have you met the need in the community you have chosen? What impact have you had on the community you have served?
- Can you gather feedback from the community you have served in order to support your ideas?
- The evaluation you have made of your community project against the criteria you have developed.
- How you have developed as a more caring and empathetic learner – the impact on yourself as an IB learner.
- How you are equipped with a greater repertoire of skill mastery that you can share with others – the impact on yourself as a self-managed learner who can support peers in their learning.

By beginning your community project presentation with the 'Why' you can draw your audience in and capture their attention from the beginning. Once they are hooked through your 'Why' you can then take them on the journey of the 'How' and explain the process of your service as action. Finally, you can provide a powerful ending through looking at the 'What', the impact on both self and others.

Presentation format 3: TED-style Talk

A TED-style Talk is a familiar approach to communicating that you can employ for your community project presentation. The goal of a TED Talk is to share ideas through a short and impactful speech. This is a meaningful way to present your community project and share your ideas, and service as action journey.

ACTIVITY: TED-STYLE TALK

The following scaffold is a general guide that you can use to ensure that you are communicating in a reflective and engaging TED-style Talk approach. How you wish to develop this is up to you. You may wish to draft this by hand, you may wish to brainstorm using both written and visual text, or you may prefer to type your presentation.

Remember, the community project is about employing your ATL skills to serve others. Use your strengths and your learning preferences to develop your presentation.

Provocation

A TED Talk tends to always begin with a provocation or a hook to capture the audience's attention and draw them in. A provocation is meant to evoke a response from your audience. It is meant to make a connection with the audience. To do this, it needs to be a universal idea that can connect with people from all walks of life. A good provocation should inspire questions and further discussion.

An example of a provocation using the following highly challenging community project goal:

Our community project goal is to create a diverse social media presence through employing appropriate and targeted hashtags with accurate and supportive information for people who are experiencing or know someone who is experiencing depression, whether it is relatively minor or severe. We wish to give people

a connection to a community they can reach out to in times of need and to also communicate ways to support those who are facing this challenge.

The provocation that this group can employ to begin their TED-style Talk presentation could be as follows:

Depression is powerful. It is often silent and unknown in our various communities; however, it is a very significant challenge that many around the world face daily. Social media can have a detrimental impact on those experiencing depression. Comments on social media sites can cause great harm to those facing such a significant challenge. As we know from the media, the harm that these comments cause can be fatal for some. We believe that we can use social media to have a positive impact on those experiencing depression. We believe that we can use social media to lessen the harm on individuals facing such a significant challenge. We chose to use social media for good, not evil.

With the provocation, you will hopefully have captured your audience's attention and have them thinking about the ideas you are presenting. Building on this, you can begin to communicate the journey of your community project from Investigating through to Taking action. Finally, communicate your reflective skills and end with your final thoughts on your community project. The following scaffold and prompt questions may be useful.

Provocation

- Capture your audience's attention – hook them and draw them into your presentation.

Investigating

Tell the story of how you investigated, this can include the following:

- An introduction to the community you are serving and the need you will address within this community. The clear and highly challenging goal you have created, the chosen global context and why, and how this is based on personal interests.
- The prior learning and subject-specific knowledge that you have identified that has been consistently highly relevant to reaching your community project goal.
- An explanation of how you have demonstrated excellent research skills, both primary and secondary, in order to learn about the community, you have served in order to address the need you have identified.

Planning

Tell the story of how you planned for service as action, this can include the following:

- An explanation of how you have developed a detailed, appropriate and thoughtful proposal for action to serve the need in the community.
- A description of how you have presented a detailed and accurate plan and record of the development process of the project.
- Examples with explanations of how you have demonstrated excellent self-management skills and how they have improved.

Taking action

Tell the story of how you placed your community project goal into action, this can include the following:

- Examples with explanations of how you have demonstrated excellent service as action as a result of the project – how you have placed your community project goal into action.
- Examples with explanations of how you have demonstrated excellent thinking skills and how they have improved.
- Examples with explanations of how you have demonstrated excellent communication and social skills and how they have improved.

Reflecting

Share your reflections on the impact of your community project and the impact of service as action on yourself as a learner, this can include the following:

- An explanation of how you have thoroughly evaluated the quality of the service as action against the proposal for action you developed in Chapter 4.
- Excellent reflections on how completing the project has extended your knowledge and understanding of service learning.
- Reflection and explanation on how you have developed approaches to learning skills.

Final thoughts

- Refer back to your provocation. Wrap up your presentation. Create a call for action. Leave your audience with ideas and questions to ponder.

Using the guiding questions from the beginning of this chapter – the content of the community project presentation – you can develop your TED-style Talk. Something to consider when developing your TED-style Talk is the following:

- The goal of a TED Talk is to spread ideas. As you share the journey of your community project, how can you ensure that this does not become simply a recount of the process, but rather an engaging communication that equips your audience with new ideas as a result of your process?

For example, if you are sharing how you have engaged in the process of critical thinking, you will want to provide anecdotes that inspire and cause your audience to think about their own critical-thinking skills.

Here is an example of this type of communication using the following community project goal: *My community project goal is to liaise with the support workers at the Migrant Centre in order to use my clothes-making skills and create new clothes for those detained at the Centre. My goal is to create clothing pieces that use materials and styles from the country of origin of those I will be creating for. The purpose of my community project goal has three parts.*

The first being, I want those at the Migrant Centre to feel welcome. Secondly, I want to show those detained that those on the other side of the Centre walls care for them. And lastly, to show an appreciation of their culture and country of origin through working with materials and styles familiar to them.

When communicating how this individual has developed critical-thinking skills using a Circle of Viewpoints thinking routine, the TED-style Talk could go a little something like this:

Now that everything was in place for me to begin creating the pieces, I had developed a pamphlet that used both English, Arabic and visual symbols to communicate options, the participants I had the honour of creating for had given their preferences, and I was ready to begin the making process. I thought this would be a fairly straightforward creation process … [pause for effect] however, part-way through I realized that I was leaning too much on style and materials, rather than the practicalities of our cold climate. So I chose to conduct a Circle of Viewpoints and testing methods, which enabled me to place myself in the position of one of the participants. I instantly realized that the focus on the materials needed to be changed, because the individual wearing this piece would be so cold once they leave the warmth of indoors. I barely made it as far as the end of our street wearing the materials before I had to run shivering to the warmth of my family's home. Therefore, I changed the design to include an inner wool liner so that materials were still used and visible, but the clothing piece was far more practical for those I was creating for. When I tested this new approach, I not only made it to the end of the street, but it was also a warm, snug and much slower journey back home.

As you can see, the critical-thinking skill has been explained, the information is presented; however, the approach is less formal and presented in a relaxed and anecdotal style. This is a key to developing an engaging and effective TED-style Talk presentation: being relaxed and drawing the audience in.

Visual aids

Visuals are often an underappreciated aspect of a presentation. Visual aids can either enhance a presentation or they can distract from it. The visual aids you choose will be a significant component of your community project presentation. This part of the chapter simply offers some tips for how to create effective visual aids to support your presentation.

What is a visual aid?

Before we launch into the types of visual aids you can employ, let's establish a shared understanding of just what visual aids are. Visual aids are essentially visual communication tools that support your presentation. For example, if you are giving a TED-style Talk you may have a Google Slide Deck behind or above you with visuals/ diagrams/process journal extracts that support your presentation. What you communicate visually on the Google Slide Deck will be your visual aid.

What can I use to create my visual aids?

There are a plethora of communication tools at your disposal in the form of software, apps and online sites that provide you with professional scaffolds. There may be some sites that you use in your other MYP subjects that you can transfer to your community project presentation.

Along with online visual aid tools, you can also use more tactile visual aid tools. You may create a pamphlet to share with your audience as a visual aid to support your presentation. You may create a prototype of a design you have created for the community you have chosen that you can present with your community project presentation.

Your school may have a specific approach to community project presentation; for example, an online school intranet that has a presentation feature may be what you are required to use. Make sure you employ your communication and social skills to ensure you clearly understand how your school structures the community project presentation.

How can I create an effective presentation?

- It is a good idea to use pictures and diagrams rather than words. Use words as infrequently as possible. The pictures and diagrams should support your oral communication. Instead of using long words, use short words instead. It is also a good idea to only use nouns, verbs and key phrases in your visual aids.

- A common presentation tip is the 'rule of 3'. If you are using bullet points in your visual aid, it is a good idea to only use 3 words per bullet point and only 3 bullet points on each page or slide of your presentation. Remember, the focus is on what you are orally communicating – the visual aids are merely a support for what you are orally communicating.

- Stick with one format or presentation style. To communicate visually in a consistent and clear manner it is a good idea to keep with the same format, colour scheme, font, size, and so on.

- When using video or audio, make sure this is short and does not consume a large part of your presentation. Make sure your video and audio are correctly embedded and you have practised making sure they work.

Remember, the community project is about you employing your strengths and talents to serve others. If you are a budding graphic designer, consider how you can use your design skills to create visual aids. If you enjoy drawing or any other visual arts medium, consider how you can create unique visual aids to complement and support your community project presentation. If you enjoy creating graphic novel-style artwork consider how you can create visual aids in this particular style. Be creative. Use your strengths and talents. Enjoy the process of creating your community project presentation.

> **EXPERT TIP**
>
> Using technology effectively provides you with multiple options for how you can communicate your visual aids. Considering the scope of choice you have in how you present your community project presentation, you can employ your creative-thinking, media literacy and communication skills to create a truly unique and innovative presentation.

Process Journal extracts

To accompany your community project presentation, you are required to submit process journal extracts. Remember, your process journal is the place where you have documented the journey of your community project from investigating through to reflecting. You should have a considerable amount of extracts to choose from.

If you have completed your community project in **a pair or a group**, you are allowed to submit a **maximum of 15 process journal extracts**.

If you have completed your community project independently you are allowed to submit a **maximum of 10 process journal extracts**.

When choosing what process journal extracts to submit it is a good idea to revisit the community project objectives and the guiding questions at the beginning of this chapter. Your process journal extracts should be organized around the community project objectives because the objectives have guided your journey throughout the community project.

Another tip for selecting process journal extracts is to reflect on your community project presentation. The following questions can guide your reflection here:

- What part of the community project can I provide further evidence of?

■ What have I addressed in my community project presentation that may be slightly lacking in depth of evidence due to time constraints?

■ What extracts can I choose to improve the evidence I have provided in my presentation?

For example, you may have shared in your community project presentation your research skills that included both primary and secondary sources; however, you may not have communicated how you have thoroughly analysed the currency, relevance, authority, accuracy and purpose of the sources. It would be a good idea to select one of your thorough analyses of sources as one of your process journal extracts to share.

Self-assessment and rehearsing

This leads us to self-assessment and rehearsing. As MYP students, you will no doubt be very familiar with self-assessment as a regular part of your school experience. Self-assessment allows you to truly take ownership of your learning and provides an opportunity for reflection and improvement.

To self-assess, pull together your community project presentation script plus the visual aids and the process journal extracts you have chosen. Then head over to Chapter 1: Understanding the community project objectives, in this book. Carefully read the community project assessment criteria and self-assess your community project presentation plus the visual aids and the process journal extracts you have chosen. The guiding questions at the beginning of this chapter are a good starting point for the self-assessment of each objective.

This should take some time and should be a reflective process. Carefully consider what you are presenting and how you can improve what you are presenting in your community project presentation. When you have finished the self-assessment process you may need to make some adjustments to your community project presentation including the visual aids and the process journal extracts you have selected.

Before you deliver your community project presentation, it is a good idea to rehearse your presentation. A rehearsal ensures that your presentation is concise and that your visual aids are complementary and enhance your presentation. An added bonus of a rehearsal is that this can increase your confidence for the actual delivery of your community project presentation. It is recommended that you rehearse your community project presentation with your supervisor in order to gather feedback. Your family and friends can also be an effective audience for rehearsal and gathering feedback; plus extra moral support from family and friends can be an added benefit.

Submission

Congratulations, you are ready to present your community project presentation and show your process of service as action. Along with your community project presentation, you need to submit the following:

An Academic honesty Form signed by both yourself and your supervisor (this will be organized through your school by the Projects Coordinator)	☐
Your proposal for action	☐
Your process journal extracts	☐
A copy of the supporting visual aids you will use in your presentation	☐
Bibliography	☐

Enjoy the opportunity to present your community project. Not only have you engaged in a sustained service as action project, but you have also significantly contributed to meeting the needs of others.

CHAPTER SUMMARY KEY POINTS

- Your community project presentation has time allocation requirements. If you have completed the community project with a partner or in a group of three, your time allocated is 10–14 minutes. If you have independently completed the community project, your time allocated is 6–10 minutes.

- Your community project needs to be organized around the community project objectives and delivered through an oral presentation.

- There are several format choices you have for presenting your community project presentation. This chapter has provided the following formats:
  - Empowering Narrative
  - Golden Circles
  - TED-style Talk.

- There are other approaches to presentations that you can take and your school will also have a repertoire for you to choose from.

- Visual aids can be used to support your community project presentation. Be sure your visual aids are creative, clear and support your oral communication.

- You can submit process journal extracts along with your presentation to provide further evidence of your community project process. If you have completed the community project with a partner or a group of three you can submit a maximum 15 pages of process journal extracts. If you have completed the community project independently, you can submit a maximum 10 pages of process journal extracts.

- It is a good idea to make the most of your self-assessment skills and to rehearse your community project presentation. This allows time for reflection and improvement before delivering your final presentation.

- At the time of presenting your community project presentation you need to submit the following:
  - Signed academic honesty form
  - Proposal for action
  - Process journal extracts
  - Supporting visual aids
  - Bibliography.

Academic honesty

ACADEMIC HONESTY

Academic honesty involves producing work which is original and, where relevant, acknowledging the work of others who have influenced your own work.

DOCUMENTS

The following tips will help you practise academic honesty in your community project:

- ✔ Submit an MYP projects academic honesty form
- ✔ Compile a bibliography
- ✔ Acknowledge all of your sources
- ✔ Be consistent in your referencing style

ACADEMIC DISHONESTY

There are many forms of academic dishonesty, but those which are most applicable to the community project are **plagiarism**, **collusion** and **fabrication**.

Academic honesty

■ ATL skills
- Communication skills
- Organization skills
- Information literacy skills
- Media literacy skills

LEARNER PROFILE ATTRIBUTES	
Inquirer	Communicator
Caring	Knowledgeable
Thinking	Principled

It is important when undertaking any type of project which involves writing or presenting to practise academic honesty. Academic honesty involves producing work which is original and, where relevant, acknowledging the work of others who have influenced your own work.

Academic honesty is a guiding principle of all academic institutions and organizations, including the IB. The philosophy of academic honesty aligns very closely with the Learner Profile. As principled learners, 'we act with integrity and honesty, with a strong sense of fairness and justice, and with respect for the dignity and rights of people everywhere. We take responsibility for our actions and their consequences'.

In today's digital age, it can be very tempting to use the ctrl-C and ctrl-V shortcut when you read something that sounds like what you want to say, but practising academic dishonesty can have serious consequences. If you are caught cheating in the IB Diploma Programme, you could risk losing your Diploma. At university level, you could potentially face expulsion. Outside of the academic world, there have been several high-profile cases of plagiarism that have led to legal proceedings. J.K. Rowling, Barack Obama and Justin Bieber have all been accused of plagiarism at some point in their careers. Even claims that are not proven have tarnished reputations.

There are many forms of academic dishonesty, but due to the nature of the community project, those that are most applicable in this context are plagiarism, collusion and fabrication.

Plagiarism: Plagiarism is using work from another source without acknowledging that source. Plagiarism may be deliberate or unintentional; either way, it is still considered 'stealing'. Any ideas which are not your own must be cited.

Collusion: Collusion is when two or more students work together on an assignment that is meant to be independent. This is different from collaboration, which is an important aspect of the approaches to learning. Collusion is a deliberate act and might involve copying from a classmate.

Fabrication: Fabrication includes inventing or misrepresenting information. This could include making up data in the experimental sciences, using fictional case studies (presented as real-life case studies) in the human sciences, or reflecting on experiences that did not happen to you.

EXPERT TIP

It is important to acknowledge that different cultures may have different attitudes towards academic honesty. Whatever your own personal views on academic honesty may be, you must follow the guidelines set out by the IB. As such, you will be expected to submit an academic honesty form, signed by your supervisor, with your proposal for action.

ACTIVITY: SPOTTING PLAGIARISM

■ ATL skills

■ Research - Information literacy skills
  • Understand and implement intellectual property rights

Read the original text source below and see if you can identify which version is an example of plagiarism.

'Service-learning is an educational approach that combines learning objectives with community service in order to provide a pragmatic, progressive learning experience while meeting societal needs'.

(En.wikipedia.org.2018)

1 Service-learning is an educational approach that combines learning objectives with community service in order to provide a pragmatic, progressive learning experience while meeting societal needs.

2 Service-learning is a way of combining learning with community service. Learning objectives are achieved by meeting the needs of society.

3 Wikipedia defines service-learning as an 'educational approach that combines learning objectives with community service in order to provide a pragmatic, progressive learning experience while meeting societal needs'.

Answers:

1 This is plagiarism. It is clearly copied word-for-word from the original text.

2 This is also plagiarism. Although the original text has been slightly reworded, the ideas are virtually the same, and this must be acknowledged.

3 This is not plagiarism because the original source has been acknowledged. However, in addition to acknowledging the source within your sentence, you would need to provide an in-text citation, which is formatted according to the style required by your school (for example., Harvard., MLA).

Citation and referencing

As with any other piece of academic coursework you complete, you must cite any sources that you have consulted, whether directly or paraphrased.

Why cite?
- To give credit to the original author(s)
- To add further support to your own claims
- To allow readers to follow up with further research using some of your sources
- To establish your own credibility as a writer

Citation

What to cite
- Any source materials or ideas which are not your own including those which are direct quotes, paraphrased or summarized.
- Written or electronic sources, online or in print
- Personal interviews

Where to cite
- In the body of your report, to distinguish between your own words and those of others
- In the bibliography or works cited page at the end of your report
- In your service as action, if appropriate

The IB does not stipulate which referencing style you use. This is up to your school. Whatever style your school expects from you (for example, Harvard, MLA, Chicago, APA), you must be consistent. There are many free websites, such as EasyBib or Citethisforme, which will help you create a bibliography that is formatted according to the referencing style your school expects.

> **EXPERT TIP**
>
> You will likely consult multiple sources throughout the research process. It is a good idea to keep a set of notecards or a digital file for each source that you consult, whether or not you end up using that information in your presentation. Organizing your information in this way will make it easier to cite your sources in your presentation; your files can also serve as a running bibliography. Refer back to Chapter 3 for more information on the evaluation of sources.

EXPERT TIP

There is a difference between a bibliography and a works cited page. A bibliography consists of all of the sources you have consulted throughout the process. A works cited includes only those sources that are directly cited in your presentation. Your community project coordinator or supervisor should be able to advise you on which format is more appropriate to your project.

Further guidance on academic honesty, citation and referencing

There are several resources available online to give you further information on academic honesty, including:

Academic Honesty in the IB educational context:

www.ibo.org/globalassets/digital-tookit/brochures/academic-honesty-ib-en.pdf

Effective citing and referencing:

www.ibo.org/globalassets/digital-tookit/brochures/effective-citing-and-referencing-en.pdf

You can also view the winning film from the IB's 2016 Academic honesty film competition (MYP), available on the IB Community Blog:

http://blogs.ibo.org/blog/2017/05/26/myp-winners-academic-honesty-film-competition/

Supervisor check-in

- Share a running bibliography with your supervisor throughout the different stages of the project.
- Consult your supervisor on when and how to appropriately cite your sources.

CHAPTER SUMMARY KEY POINTS

- Academic honesty must be practised throughout the process, and all sources must be acknowledged according to recognized conventions.

- Keep track of all of your sources as you engage in the research process.

- You will be required to submit an academic honesty form with your proposal for action. This form will need to be signed by your supervisor to authenticate your work.

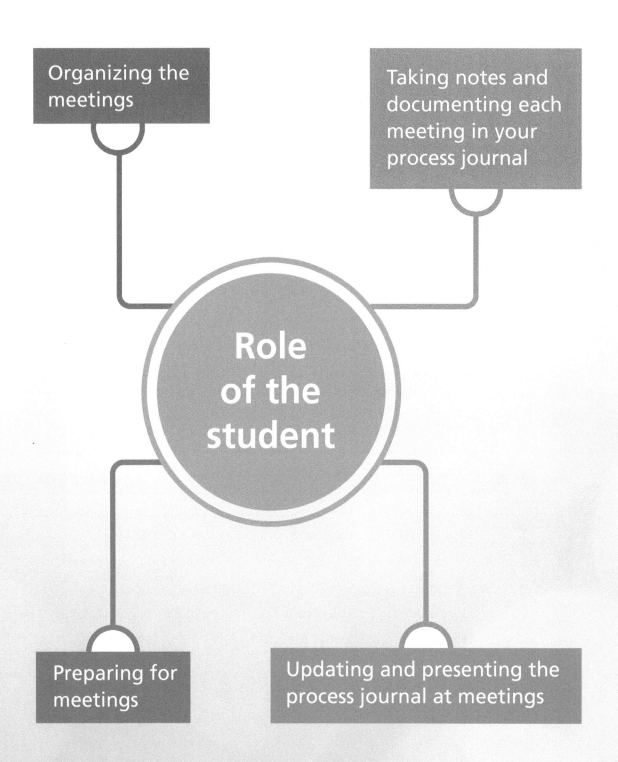

Organizing the meetings

Taking notes and documenting each meeting in your process journal

Role of the student

Preparing for meetings

Updating and presenting the process journal at meetings

the supervisor

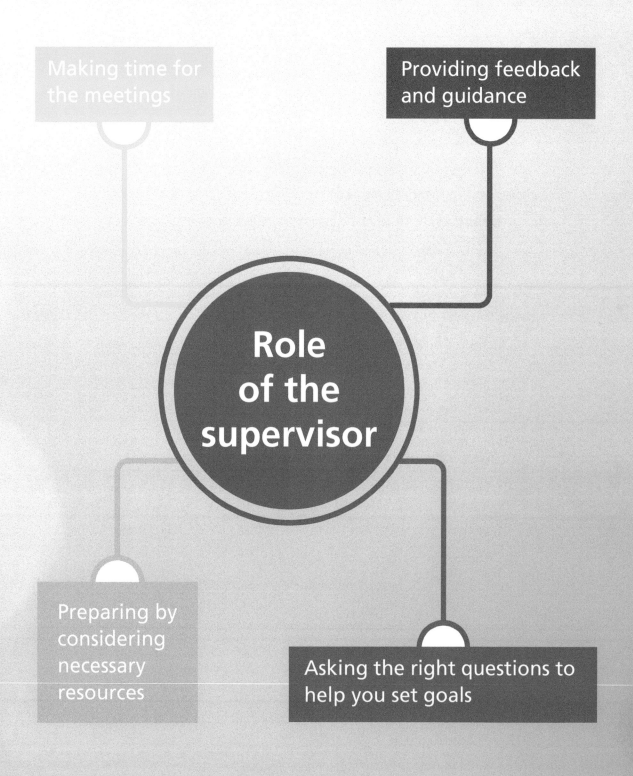

Making time for the meetings

Providing feedback and guidance

Role of the supervisor

Preparing by considering necessary resources

Asking the right questions to help you set goals

The role of the supervisor

ATL skills

- Communication skills
- Collaboration skills
- Reflection skills

LEARNER PROFILE ATTRIBUTES

Communicator	Open-minded	Balanced

This chapter outlines the 'Why, What and How' of the role of your community project supervisor and your interaction with them.

Why does the IB require community project students to have a supervisor?

As the community project is an independent and self-managed project that does not form part of your MYP subject areas, your allocated supervisor is your support person to help you manage the community project independently and develop self-management skills outside of an MYP subject area classroom.

Support, collaboration and feedback are important for all projects, both at school and beyond. The community project is a significant project that requires support, collaboration and feedback in order for you to experience the benefits of service as action. Your supervisor is crucial as this support person is a key person to collaborate with and to provide you with timely, strategic and descriptive feedback.

What is the role of your community project supervisor?

The community project supervisor is primarily a support role. Your community project supervisor is your one-person cheer squad so your community project experience can be an experience that empowers you to flourish and grow as a self-managed learner.

The supervisor's responsibilities:

- Ensure that the proposal for action you have chosen satisfies appropriate legal and ethical standards with regard to health and safety, confidentiality, human rights, animal welfare and environmental issues.

- Provide guidance and feedback throughout each part of the community project inquiry cycle.

- In the community project meetings that you organize, they will coach you through your community project to help you become an increasingly self-managed and self-directed learner.

- At the end of your community project journey, they will confirm the authenticity of your work and through a standardization process, mark your community project against the MYP community project criteria.

You will receive information and guidance from your supervisor that may include:

- guides about the community project
- a timetable with deadlines
- the assessment criteria for the project
- advice on how to keep and use your process journal
- the importance of personal analysis and reflection
- formative feedback
- requirements for academic honesty.

Your school will set up the supervisor process, allocations and the sharing of community project guiding information in ways that best suit your school context.

How can your community project supervisor provide support, collaboration and feedback?

Your responsibility: Organizing the meeting

Employing your communication, media literacy and social skills, you will need to contact your supervisor for an appropriate and regular time to meet. Your meetings are a time for you to collaboratively discuss these ideas and your progress and for your supervisor to provide you with feedback.

Once a time has been confirmed along with a location, make sure you send your supervisor a meeting request so this meeting is added to their busy calendars.

Ensure you come prepared and ready to share, reflect and receive feedback. Your process journal needs to be present at your community project meetings. Make sure you take notes and document each meeting in your process journal as evidence of your communication and social skills.

Supervisor's responsibility: Engaging in the meeting

At your meetings with your supervisor, they will ask you how you are progressing and read through, or listen to, sections of your process journal. They will give you feedback and guidance based on what you have shared with them and ensure that you have the tools to go further.

A great tool to provide your supervisor with at the community project meetings is the GROWTH model question starters. These question starters will help you unpack just where you are currently in your community project at the time of the meeting, break down what needs to happen and help you set goals as a result of the support, collaboration and feedback your supervisor has given you.

> **G** – Goals: What do you need to achieve?
> **R** – Reality: What is happening now?
> **O** – Options: What could you do?
> **W** – Will: What will you do?
> **T** – Tactics: How and when will you do it?
> **H** – Habits: How will you sustain your success?

Make sure you connect with your supervisor regularly and reflect on your meetings and interactions with them in your process journal. Your supervisor is your one-person cheer squad throughout the process of the community project, so take their ideas and feedback on board and grow as an increasingly effective communicator and self-managed learner throughout the process.

ACTIVITY: ELICITING QUALITY FEEDBACK – WHAT WENT WELL/EVEN BETTER IF

ATL skills

- Collaboration skills
  - Give and receive meaningful feedback
- Reflection skills
  - Identify the strengths and weaknesses of personal learning strategies (self-assessment)

Feedback should be a dialogue between you and your supervisor. As an active learner, you have as much of a responsibility as they do in the feedback process, so don't be shy in approaching your supervisor for specific feedback on how to meet the community project objectives.

You may be familiar with the feedback strategy *What Went Well (WWW)/Even Better If (EBI)*. If this is a new strategy for you, it is simply a way of judging the quality of your work by highlighting strengths and making suggestions for improvements. If your supervisor does not offer this kind of feedback on their own, try asking for it at one of your meetings. You could even self-assess (individually or as a group) before your meeting and see how your assessment compares with your supervisor's. Try to be as specific as possible and remember to refer to the assessment criteria. Alternatively, you could take the feedback you have already been given and view it through the WWW/EBI lens.

What Went Well (WWW) ...	Even Better If (EBI) ...

EXPERT TIP

When you invest a lot of time and effort into a project, it's easy to react emotionally when you get feedback that can be perceived as negative. It is important to remember that your supervisor is on your side, and it is their job to ensure that you achieve the best possible outcome.

Managing the process and your time

Tips for successfully managing your time:

1 Create a realistic plan.

2 Re-evaluate throughout. Does your plan need adjusting? Are some tasks taking more or less time than you anticipated?

3 Checklists can help you keep track of your progress:

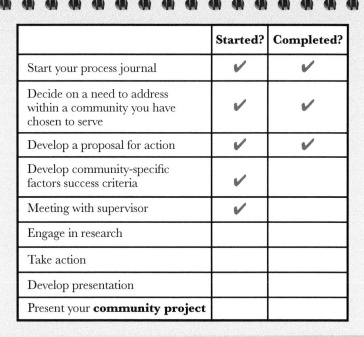

	Started?	Completed?
Start your process journal	✔	✔
Decide on a need to address within a community you have chosen to serve	✔	✔
Develop a proposal for action	✔	✔
Develop community-specific factors success criteria	✔	
Meeting with supervisor	✔	
Engage in research		
Take action		
Develop presentation		
Present your **community project**		

4 Remember to take breaks every now and then, and practise mindfulnes.

Managing the process and your time

LEARNER PROFILE ATTRIBUTES

Balanced	Principled	Caring

Growing as a balanced learner requires intentional planning, reflection and organization. Balanced learners understand the importance of balancing different aspects of their lives – intellectually, physically and emotionally – to achieve well-being for themselves and others.

As MYP students there are no doubt multiple commitments and responsibilities that require your focus and time. Some of them might be:

■ school

■ homework

■ study for examinations

■ clubs

■ sporting groups

■ community engagement.

Just to name a few …

And of course, time with family, friends, pursuing hobbies and side projects, engaging in various social media platforms and relaxing downtime to recharge is of utmost importance and needs to be considered and prioritized.

In MYP Year 3 or 4, added to this list is the community project.

These can require a significant amount of juggling and can become overwhelming if not managed wisely.

A tool to support you and ensure that you do not become overwhelmed is to prioritize just what is required of you. Prioritization is a skill that requires reflection and planning ahead.

KEY WORD

Prioritize is a verb, an action word. To prioritize is something you need to actively do. To prioritize means to determine the order that you will address just what is required of you. Prioritizing your workload is a continual, reflective process.

One way of helping you prioritize and manage the community project process and time is through to-do lists. To-do lists are such a simple and yet effective means of organizing the various aspects of your school life and the process of your community project.

Choose strategic points throughout the process – this may be each week, fortnightly or monthly. It is up to you and your prioritization needs when you choose these strategic points. Use a planning method that best suits your approach to learning; for example, a diary, an online calendar with set notifications and reminders, your chosen planning method from Chapter 4, and so on. It is important that the planning method you choose is the preferred planning method that you are comfortable with.

Using this planning method, create your to-do list by simply jotting down in bullet point form what you need to achieve within the time frame you have set. Once you have jotted this down, allocate a numerical prioritization order or highlight the most important to least important to help you visualize and organize just what you need to achieve.

Make sure you include strategic meeting times with your community project supervisor so that you can receive the best possible support and further develop your social and communication skills.

Tick these off as you complete each of these tasks, as this will help you remain positive and continual bursts of accomplishment will help you effectively engage in the community project and meet the need of the community you are serving to the best of your ability.

Key to community project success is prioritizing your workload. Forward planning and prioritization means you won't leave the community project to the last minute and consequently experience unnecessary stress and be overwhelmed.

Remember to pause every once in a while, close or shut down your devices and head outdoors or to a quiet location to unwind, rest your body and mind and recharge. Take the time to reflect, be mindful and be still. Time to pause is crucial to effectively manage your process and time, as this demonstrates how you are growing as a balanced learner who understands the importance of balancing the intellectual, physical and emotional aspects of their life.

CHAPTER SUMMARY KEY POINTS

- The community project is an ongoing piece of work, so you need to manage your time well.

- Re-evaluate your priorities throughout the process.

- Create a checklist of tasks so you can keep track of what you have completed, and what still needs to be done.

- Remember to take time out every now and then.

Appendix

Top 10 tips from the authors

1 Choose a need in a community you are passionate about. Your involvement in the community project and contribution to the community you are serving can have the potential to establish a lasting connection.

2 If you are intending to complete the community project with a partner or as a group of three, make sure you choose fellow students who are hardworking and have complementary strengths to you.

3 Connect with your community project supervisor right at the beginning of the community project. Your supervisor will be crucial for successful service as action.

4 Use every opportunity available to ask for – and act on – constructive feedback from your supervisor, members of the community that you are serving and your peers.

5 During the research process make sure you connect with the community you are serving as much as possible. The information and feedback you receive directly from the community will be of great benefit as you place your community project goal into action.

6 Use the process journal for its intended purpose: as a tool that charts your development. The process journal is an integral part in your community project: if you view it as such, and not as additional work, then you will reap the benefits.

7 Keep a running bibliography of sources that you consult during the process; this includes 'human' resources as well as more traditional sources like books, journals, websites, and so on. Keeping a list will make life easier when it comes time to compile your bibliography.

8 If you are working on the community project with a group, communicate openly and honestly – and often – with the members of your group. If something isn't working for you, say so. The success of the group depends on each individual's contribution. You should be supportive of one another but being supportive does not mean picking up someone else's slack.

9 Embrace all opportunities for learning, even mistakes and failures. The community project is an opportunity for you to develop resilience so that you are better prepared to take on the next challenges in your academic journey.

10 The community project is also an opportunity to engage in a truly holistic experience. A holistic experience enables you to emotionally, intellectually and physically connect with what you are learning. Consider the ways in which you can enhance your learning experiences in your MYP subjects with a similar approach.

Index